Nineteen Jumps and a Prayer

Travis Monday

Nineteen Jumps and a Prayer

By Travis Monday

ISBN 978-0-6151-6350-5

Copyright 2007 by Travis Monday; 2nd Edition 2010

Online editions may also be available for this title. For more information, please visit www.lulu.com.

All rights reserved. No part of this book may be reproduced or transmitted in any form or by any means without permission by the author.

"Scripture quotations marked (NASB) are taken from the New American Standard Bible®, Copyright © 1960, 1962, 1963, 1968, 1971, 1972, 1973, 1975, 1977, 1995 by The Lockman Foundation Used by permission." (www.Lockman.org)

"Scripture quotations marked (NLT) are taken from the *Holy Bible*, New Living Translation, copyright © 1996. Used by permission of Tyndale House Publishers, Inc., Wheaton, Illinois 60189. All rights reserved."

Printed in the United States of America

Dedication

I dedicate this book to all the men and women who served our nation in the Vietnam War and to the family members and friends who supported them.

Preface to 2nd Edition

Part of the blame for my decision to write the story of my military service goes to Rodney Watson, who graduated with me from Plainview High School in Plainview, Texas, as part of the Class of 1970. While I signed books in Plainview one evening, he stopped by and asked me to write down my experiences for the Museum of the Llano Estacado's Hale County Veteran Survey.

I had already thought about writing my autobiography, so Watson's request strengthened my conviction that the time was right. The decision to create this 2nd Edition is motivated by a need to correct a few mistakes and to add some additional information.

Another factor in my initial decision to write this book was my wife Pam's decision to go skydiving, and my two sons' decisions to join her.

Writing my own life story proved both difficult and therapeutic. I've confessed to a good bit of personal wrongdoing and have sought to share my failures as well as my successes.

Something else I've done is to use my journey as a vehicle for telling stories about others. I am honored to help preserve the history of friends and relatives and other people whose lives have in some way intersected with mine – either directly or indirectly.

I've also attempted to preserve some military and regional history that might not survive otherwise.

My story consists of more than a mere series of military experiences as a paratrooper in the U. S. Army. It includes my spiritual journey and the difference that Jesus Christ has made in my life. More than anything else, I pray that my story will honor him.

Travis Monday
May 16, 2010
San Angelo, Texas

Table of Contents

You'd Have to Be Crazy! 1
Parachutes and Patriotism 13
Basic Combat Training 35
Lost-in-the-Woods Leadership 51
Airborne Mechanic? 57
The Grind of Ground Week 67
Those Terrific Towers 79
The Joy of Jump Week 89
America -- Love It *Then* Leave It 99
Delta Developers -- Part 1 109
Delta Developers -- Part 2 131
Screaming Eagles in Vietnam 143
An Eagle with Sky Soldiers 159
From Airborne to Chairborne 177
Airborne Again! 191
After Airborne 211
Adios Airborne 249
My Jumping Jack Family 257
Bibliography 267
Index 272

You'd Have to Be Crazy!

Figure 1 Travis Monday in Jump School at Fort Benning, Georgia (Author's collection; Winter, 1971).

"You'd have to be crazy to jump out of a perfectly good airplane!" That's what other soldiers told me when they found out I'd volunteered for the U. S. Army's Airborne School, also known as "Jump School."

Me crazy? Maybe. And maybe jumping out of an airplane would prove it. But crazy or not, I didn't intend to change my mind after two weeks of Airborne training at Fort Benning, Georgia.

Waiting on the Runway

Figure 2 Airborne trainees boarding a Fairchild C-119 Flying Boxcar at Fort Benning, Georgia (U. S. Army photo).

Before long I'd make my first jump, but first I had to sit on the runway with the other volunteers and wait for the arrival of a Fairchild C-119 Flying Boxcar.

You'll never guess what we had to listen to while we waited – a song called "Blood on the Risers." A rather sadistic sounding title, don't you think?

Of course, you need to hear some of the words before making up your mind about the song itself. The singers in the recording sang to the tune of "The Battle Hymn of the Republic."

> He was just a rookie trooper,
> And he surely shook with fright
> As he checked all his equipment,
> And made sure his pack was tight.
> He had to sit and listen
> To those awful engines roar,
> You ain't gonna jump no more.
>
> Gory, gory, what a helluva way to die.
> Gory, gory, what a helluva way to die.
> Gory, gory, what a helluva way to die.
> He ain't gonna jump no more!

Just as a reminder, we listened to this encouraging piece of musical artistry while waiting to make our first jump.

Since the song is rather lengthy, I'm only sharing part of it and I've chosen not to repeat the chorus at the end of each stanza.

> Is everyone happy?
> Cried the sergeant looking up,
> Our Hero feebly answered "Yes,"
> And then they stood him up.
> He leaped right out into the blast,
> His static line unhooked,
> He ain't gonna jump no more!
>
> He counted long, he counted loud,
> He waited for the shock,
> He felt the wind, he felt the clouds,
> He felt the awful drop,
> He jerked his cord, the silk spilled out
> And wrapped around his legs,
> He ain't gonna jump no more!

Now, if you're a bit squeamish, you might want to skip the next couple of stanzas. *YOU'VE BEEN WARNED!*

> He hit the ground, the sound was "Splat,"
> His blood went spurting high.
> His comrades then were heard to say,
> "A helluva way to die."
> He lay there rolling 'round
> In the welter of his gore.
> He ain't gonna jump no more!
>
> There was blood upon the risers,
> There were brains upon the 'Chute;
> Intestines were a'dangling
> From his Paratrooper's boots
> They picked him up, still in his 'Chute
> And poured him from his boots.
> He ain't gonna jump no more!

Listening to that song while waiting to make my first parachute jump made me think that maybe jumping out of an airplane meant I really was a bit crazy.

No one ever explained to me the psychology of playing "Blood on the Risers" to a bunch of Airborne trainees waiting to make their first jump. Perhaps playing that song under those circumstances helped us face our worst fears and even laugh at them. Paratroopers need to learn to laugh at their fears, including their fear of death.

Take Off!

Figure 3 Fairchild C-119 Flying Boxcar in flight (U. S. Air Force photo).

Whoever came up with the idea of jumping out of "a *perfectly good* airplane" probably never took off in an old worn out C-119. The vibrations gave me the feeling that I'd rather *jump* out of that plane than *land* in it.

I felt considerable relief when the airplane finally made it off the ground.

My first experience of flying in a propeller-driven aircraft felt different than flying in a jet airliner. Earlier I had flown in a jet from Texas to California on my way to Fort Ord for Basic Training.

Ten Minute Warning

After we'd been in the air for a while, the man they call the Jumpmaster faced us, stuck his arms out in front of him with his thumbs and all his fingers extended upwards and shouted, "Ten minutes!" He had to shout because of the noise of the engines. Using hand signals reinforced his efforts to let us know we would jump soon.

While I may not be telling you all of this in the exact order of occurrence, I want you to know that the Jumpmaster occasionally updated us on the time. He yelled, "Five minutes!" Then, "Four minutes!" And so on. With each passing minute the knot in my stomach got tighter and the lump in my throat got bigger.

Get Ready!

At one point the Jumpmaster stood before us and shouted, "Get ready!" Get ready for what? Get ready to make final preparations for your jump and get ready for the jump itself.

Why did we need to get ready? Because our lives depended on faithfully following the commands we would soon receive.

Stand Up!

Another thing the Jumpmaster says on the way to the DZ (Drop Zone) is, "Stand Up!" Standing up might not seem all that important if you've never made a military parachute jump, but our training included learning how to make a stand-up exit from a moving aircraft.

Standing up could prove difficult when wearing a parachute and harness and a reserve parachute, especially when you hadn't had much practice and when the movement of the airplane made keeping your balance somewhat of a challenge. You've heard of sailors getting their "sea legs." Well, we hadn't yet developed our "air legs."

Figure 4 Airborne students inside of an airplane waiting to make a jump (U. S. Army photo).

Hook Up!

After we stood up our Jumpmaster shouted, "Hook up!" As he gave the command he used his index fingers to make the shape of a hook and simulated a hooking movement. Static line jumps differ from skydiving because the parachute-opening mechanism activates your parachute as you leave the aircraft. With skydiving the jumper pulls a ripcord after first freefalling for a while.

Our static lines consisted of yellow nylon-looking straps with locking metal hooks on the end. We hooked our static lines to metal cables that ran from the rear of the aircraft forward like a clothesline in a back yard.

Check Equipment!

Hooking up our static lines set the stage for another command, "Check equipment!" Why would you want to check your equipment? Because you didn't want to die!

Actually, you didn't check all of your own equipment. Instead, you would check the equipment on the front side of your body while the guy in line behind you checked the parachute on your back. It just didn't pay to make enemies in an Airborne unit because your life might depend on they guy you hacked off.

The Jumpmaster would then say, "Sound off for equipment check!" Starting at the back of the line, each soldier, if his equipment seemed safe, would yell, "Okay!" while he also tapped the guy in front of him on the thigh -- the signal that it was his turn to sound off next. Down the line it would go until the message got back to the Jumpmaster.

Stand in the Door!

We had a signal light in the aircraft that changed from red to green. I'm sure you know that green means "Go!" Before the first aspiring paratrooper actually left our C-119, the Jumpmaster shouted, "Stand in the door!" By that time the door had already been opened, so the noise of the engines and the wind made it hard to hear much else.

As commanded, the guys at the front of the line on each side of the aircraft took their place standing in the door. They would soon receive the command, "Go!" Next, they would intentionally leave the safety of the aircraft in order to take their chances with a parachute. In keeping with their training, they would exit the aircraft and assume a body position intended to keep them from tumbling wildly through the sky before their parachutes opened.

Waiting for My Turn

In the type of military jump I was about to make, the jumpers were organized into groups known as sticks. In essence a stick consisted of a group of jumpers in a line organized for a jump.

On the day I made my first jump, I stood near the back end of my stick, so while waiting for my turn I watched other men exit the aircraft ahead of me. Each time a man in our stick went out the door, the rest of us would step forward in a movement known as the "Airborne Shuffle."

I'll have to admit that during this waiting and watching process I had some second thoughts. As each man stepped up to the door and made his exit, it seemed as if the powerful winds created by the blast of the propellers had sucked him out into eternity – never to be seen again.

Watching this process while moving closer and closer to the door made the knot in my stomach even tighter and the lump in my throat even larger.

Exiting the Aircraft

When I stepped up to the door to make my first jump, the anxiety became almost unbearable.

Since all of us were making our first jump, the Jumpmaster tapped each of us on the thigh and shouted "Go!" after we took our position standing in the door.

As instructed during my earlier training, I made a vigorous leap out of the aircraft expecting a collision with the wind blast from the nearest propeller. I was not disappointed. The only other time I had felt a wind blast like that had been during a tornado in Lubbock, Texas, during my childhood. On that occasion I didn't think I would make it from a car to a storm cellar, but somehow I did.

Exiting the aircraft with vigor reduced the likelihood of being blown up against the fuselage of the airplane. Because of the design of the C-119, that probably wouldn't happen.

Another part of properly exiting the aircraft consisted of assuming a tight body position and waiting for the opening shock of the parachute. We had to count to four in this manner: "One thousand. Two thousand. Three thousand. Four thousand."

For the record, I didn't yell "Geronimo!" as I went out the door.

Opening Shock

The opening shock of the parachute didn't hurt at all. I had expected it to hurt as it had during some of the training I had received during the first two weeks of Jump School.

I welcomed the opening shock since it meant my parachute had opened.

Check Canopy

In behalf of the canopy of the parachute I would like to say, "The canopy can!" It *can* support the weight of a human body.

After counting to four and feeling the opening shock of the parachute, I checked my canopy and found it fully opened. What a beautiful sight!

Descent

Remember all that anxiety I suffered while in the aircraft? Well, as I went out the door, the anxiety disappeared. I visually checked my canopy and found it in good shape and enjoyed the sensation of descent. I loved the feeling of riding a parachute.

The delight of descent increased as I enjoyed the view.

Although I loved the sensation of descending and the beauty of the view, I had to remember my training. Other jumpers shared the sky with me and we had to watch out for each other. If we got too close to another jumper or another jumper got too close to us, we'd yell, "Slip away!" By pulling on our risers in certain ways we could change the direction of our drift and avoid collisions.

Landing

At an altitude of about one hundred feet, I prepared to land by noting the direction of my movement, by slipping into the wind, and by positioning my body for a parachute landing fall (PLF). My instructors had trained me well and I made a perfect PLF and suffered no injuries.

We had taken off in our C-119 in Georgia, but we had jumped into Alabama. That means that I made my first visit to Alabama at the bottom of a parachute.

Packed Up and Picked Up

Figure 5 A jumper gathers his parachute after a jump (U. S. Army photo).

Even with a good PLF a jumper couldn't afford to just lie on the ground resting. I jumped to my feet and collapsed my canopy so that the wind couldn't drag me away. I then rolled up my parachute and harness and put them in an Army-issued bag.

After packing up, I expected to get picked up, but first I had to walk to the assembly area where the trucks sat waiting for us. The exhilaration of making my first jump made walking to the assembly area a breeze.

Reaction to My First Jump

Completing my first parachute jump left me overjoyed. I thought I would like parachuting and I did.

Because of some things that happened in Basic Training, I had lost faith in the Army, but the excellent training I received in Jump School restored some of that faith.

As I walked off the drop zone, I felt good about joining the Army and looked forward to getting my wings. You see, one jump does not a paratrooper make.

Parachutes and Patriotism

Figure 6 President John F. Kennedy (left) with future president Lyndon B. Johnson.

"Ask not what your country can do for you;
ask what you can do for your country."
--President John F. Kennedy

"Back at home the war was protested
while in the jungles our men were tested."
--Travis Monday

Before we resume the story of my adventures as an Army paratrooper, allow me to explain how I ended up joining the Army and volunteering for Airborne.

Why Parachutes?

Parachutes have always fascinated me. Even my childhood efforts at drawing stick figures included soldiers wearing parachutes. By the time I became a teenager I had already jumped off the roof of a house. When some friends and I built a set of cardboard wings and climbed to the roof, guess who volunteered to test them first? That's right – I did.

In case you're wondering, our homemade wings didn't work.

When a television series called *Ripcord* began airing episodes about skydiving, it captured my attention and energized my imagination.

Flag Fever

My fascination with parachutes developed along side of a patriotic spirit. While living in Floydada, Texas, an ex-Marine named Mr. Waller taught my fifth grade class. Some of his patriotism rubbed off on me.

Through Mr. Waller's influence I entered an essay contest about our nation's flag. The local newspaper printed some of the essays, including mine. With a couple of corrections but no major changes, here is what I wrote:

> The flag when it is unfurled makes me think of the United States of America. And the men who gave their lives for our country.
>
> It makes me feel proud. I can't really put my feelings toward the flag in words. It is kind of a good warm feeling right down in my heart.
>
> I think of the states the flag's stars stand for.
>
> I think of the other countries that fought on our side.
>
> I think of all the colonies and people in them and all their troubles that they went through just to settle the United States of America.
>
> I think of America our great nation. Our free country. I think of freedom, justice and liberty. The home of the brave. And the land of the free.

After my family moved from Floydada to Plainview, Texas, one of my English teachers made us memorize poems and recite them in class. A World War I poem by John McCrae called "In Flanders Field" further inspired my patriotic spirit.

> In Flanders fields the poppies blow
> Between the crosses row on row,
> That mark our place; and in the sky
> The larks, still bravely singing, fly
> Scarce heard amid the guns below.
>
> We are the Dead. Short days ago
> We lived, felt dawn, saw sunset glow,
> Loved and were loved, and now we lie
> In Flanders fields.
>
> Take up our quarrel with the foe:
> To you from failing hands we throw
> The torch; be yours to hold it high.
> If ye break faith with us who die
> We shall not sleep, though poppies grow
> In Flanders fields.

McCrae's concept of the dead speaking to the living helped set the stage for a lifetime of speculation – speculation about what the dead would say to the living if given the opportunity.

And other works, including songs about our nation, also contributed to my patriotic tendencies. I grew up believing in America and admiring Americans who served our country in the military.

Jimmy Dean

Soon after we moved into a farm house a few miles east of the Seth Ward area of Plainview, my mother took me to get a haircut in the home of Ruth Dean, the mother of the famous entertainer and future sausage king, Jimmy Dean.

In his autobiography, *Thirty Years of Sausage, Fifty Years of Ham*, Dean speaks of his mother cutting hair for fifteen cents.[1] Many years later, when she cut my hair, the price had gone up to seventy-five cents, but most barbers charged a lot more.

I never met Jimmy Dean, but once while Mrs. Dean was cutting my hair she received a telephone call from him. After she hung up she said proudly, "That was my son, Jimmy."

Figure 7 W. B. Monday, Jr., who graduated from Plainview High School in Plainview, Texas, on May 28, 1948, went to high school with the famed entertainer and sausage-maker, Jimmy Dean (Author's collection).

My dad, W. B. Monday, Jr., went to school with Jimmy and with his brother, Don. When I asked what he remembered about Jimmy he replied:

> He was a senior when I was a junior. His brother, Don, was in the same grade as me. The memory I have of Jimmy is that he was always fun to be around, cutting up but not boisterous. Just a

---

[1] Jimmy Dean and Donna Meade Dean, *Thirty Years of Sausage, Fifty Years of Ham: Jimmy Dean's Own Story* (New York: Berkley Books, 2004), 8.

good kid who grew up in Seth Ward where we lived at one time. His mother cut hair in her home to provide for her sons. Jimmy was a hard worker and never did anything to embarrass his mother.

My sister, Teressa, worked in a Jimmy Dean sausage plant in Plainview. She mostly dealt with Don and could not remember much about Jimmy.

You may wonder what Jimmy Dean has to do with my patriotic tendencies. Let me explain. While many folks associate Dean primarily with his hit song, "Big John," he also had a hit called, "PT-109." In "PT-109" he told the story of John F. Kennedy's experiences as the commander of a PT boat in the Pacific Ocean in World War II. The song helped me develop admiration for men who served their country in the military.

While I'm on the topic of JFK, he said something that strengthened my patriotic spirit: "Ask not what your country can do for you; ask what you can do for your country."

Monday Family Influence

I've already mentioned my dad's association with Jimmy and Don Dean. Although he never served in the military, I remember Dad as a patriot, and his patriotism influenced me.

Dad's father and my grandfather, W. B. Monday, Sr., told me about riding horseback to enter the Army in World War I. Before he arrived at the induction center he received word that the war had ended.

Dad's brother and my uncle, Joe Monday, made a career out of the U. S. Navy. On July 29, 1967, he survived the disaster on the USS Forrestal aircraft carrier off the coast of Vietnam. Fires and explosions took the lives of one hundred and thirty-four of his fellow sailors, and injured many more.

Senator John S. McCain, a Navy pilot at the time, barely escaped with his life when a rocket on an F-4 Phantom accidentally fired and hit McCain's A-4 Skyhawk. Although he suffered minor injuries from shrapnel, McCain managed to escape from his aircraft just in time to avoid a series of major explosions.

Figure 8 The author's uncle, Joe Monday, helped fight the fires that resulted from a series of explosions on board the USS Forrestal aircraft carrier off the coast of Vietnam on July 29, 1967 (U. S. Navy photo).

Joe later shared with me some of his memories of that disaster:

> There was a Chief Petty Officer from the ship who went out there with a fire extinguisher to try to extinguish the fire before it got too bad. They never found anything of him but the shoes.
> We got up and finally found our way forward. The fire actually started on the aft part of the carrier. We had just got off a 12-hour shift and had been sleeping over an hour, and we went to our respective squadrons to try to help.

Water was getting in to where the batteries were. When batteries and sea water get together you've got chlorine gas. Four people died from that.

We lost in our squadron, DF11, thirty-six men. Our sister squadron, DF74, lost thirty-four men.

Joe later visited me in Vietnam, but I'll say more about that later.

Figure 9 Joe Monday made a career out of serving his country in the U. S. Navy (Author's collection).

Williams Family Influence

My mother's maiden name is Williams, and three of her brothers served our country in the military during World War II. Johnny Lawrence Williams served as a machine gunner in the Army in the Pacific, winning some medals in the process. By way of a V-Mail sent to Mother, he wrote, "If the war don't hurry up over on this side, Germany with its army will be wiped out before we are through with the Japs. I thought we would help lick the Germans, but it looks like the other way around now."

Another of Mother's brothers, Richard L. Williams, Jr., served in the Air Corps from 1942 to 1945 with the A.S.N. Night Fighters Squadron.

The other Williams brother, L. J., served in the Pacific on the USS Alpine, a destroyer transport. His ship sustained two hits by kamikaze pilots who intentionally crashed their airplanes into the ship.

Two Step Dads

Since I'm on the topic of family influences, let me mention my two step dads – Billy C. Green and N. G. Phillips, who both served in the military. Bill served with the U.S. Army in Korea and Glynn served with the Army on Guadalcanal in World War II. They, too, contributed to my patriotism through the stories they told me about their experiences as soldiers.

Sports Influences

The patriotism that developed within me included a strong desire to win, and part of that desire grew out of sports. During my freshman year at Plainview High School, I got a good taste of winning while playing second string fullback on the Blue Pups football team. Although I never beat out Ronny Fudge for the first string position, I shared the team's pride when Coach Priest led us through an undefeated season – a perfect 10-0 record.

While playing second string on the Blue Pups, I also played first string on the Purple Pups – a team consisting of second-string players from the Blue Pups and the Red Pups. I know that sounds a bit strange, but *I'm not making this up.* My big moment with the Purple Pups came when a block by Rudy Rangel enabled me to take a handoff and run with the ball for a seventy-five yard gain.

Another high point in my Plainview sports experience came during a city track meet between Estacado Junior High and Coronado Junior High. While running for Coronado, I won first place in the 440-yard dash.

During my high school years I knew a lot of winners, including Jerry Sisemore, who later played professional football for the Philadelphia Eagles. Jerry eventually made it into the Texas Sports Hall of Fame Museum in Waco.

In P. E. (Physical Education) in Plainview we sometimes played "King of the Mat." Jerry usually won those battles, but I enjoyed being one of the last people he'd throw off. The main thing I had going for me against bigger guys with greater strength was my speed. When they'd catch me, I'd get real slippery real fast.

Vocational Industrial Clubs of America

Figure 10 Plainview High School officers in Vocational Industrial Clubs of America (VICA). Left to right -- Front: Mike Thompson and Auto Mechanics instructor Cleo Savage; Left to right -- Back: Travis Monday, Randy Keeling, and David Ware (Author's collection).

Vocational Industrial Clubs of America (VICA) also played an important part in helping me develop a love for winning along with a love for my country. Mr. Cleo Savage helped instill those kinds of values in those of us who went through his Auto Mechanics Class. At the time I didn't know it, but Mr. Savage's instruction in auto mechanics would strongly affect my Army experience.

Through Mr. Savage's influence, David Ware and I got involved in VICA during our last two years of high school. That first year Ware got the job of District VI parliamentarian while I served as a District VI delegate. From Electrical Trades Class in Plainview, Robert Hernandez served as state parliamentarian and Tom Quintanilla as District VI sergeant-at-arms. While in Austin for a state leadership conference, we attended a session of the state senate and received official recognition from Lt. Governor Ben Barnes.

At the local level, I served Auto Mechanics Chapter 328 as reporter, and that experience helped push me closer toward my goal of becoming a writer. Ware served as parliamentarian and Mike Thompson as president.

The following year Ware served as chapter president and I assisted him as vice-president. I got another good taste of winning when our local chapter was named Outstanding Auto Mechanics Chapter of Texas at the state convention in Austin. Ware outdid himself when he won the title Outstanding VICA Student of Texas. While in Austin for the state leadership conference earlier that same year, we met Governor Preston Smith in the capitol building.

Before leaving Austin, I made a patriotic speech expressing my support for our soldiers in Vietnam, and the negative response of some of those in the audience surprised me.

Antiwar Influences

Many of my friends viewed Vietnam as a mistake, and I did not hate them for it. Sometimes I also questioned the war, but I admired those who put their lives on the line for America and for the freedom of the South Vietnamese.

Freedom

If America is about anything, it is about freedom.

Figure 11 Drawing by the author as a 6-year-old child showing paratroopers in battle.

In reviewing some of my childhood artwork, I found a picture of a battle I had drawn in the first grade using stick figures for soldiers. I had named the picture, "The Battle of Freedom Hill." The drawing may have been inspired by Gregory Peck's movie about the Korean War called *Pork Chop Hill*. To me war meant fighting for freedom – including the freedom to survive. I was born in Odessa, Texas, in June of 1952 – during the Korean War.

In another childhood drawing of a battle I added soldiers with parachutes descending from the sky, so my interest in paratroopers dates back to the early years of my life.

During an earlier war, the Texas War of Independence, men in the Alamo fought for freedom. On the day before his death, Alamo commander William Barrett Travis prepared a last desperate message appealing for help from Colonel Fannin, commander of the Texas troops at Goliad. He said to his messenger, James Allen: "James, from Goliad go to all the colonies. Tell the people Texas can be a republic, but it will require greater courage to declare for independence than to stand defiantly in these old walls and die. And remember, James, whatever happens, wherever you go, carry this message forth – freedom rests finally upon those willing to die for it."[2]

You might want to call me an Alamo addict because I never tire of that topic. Even my name connects me to the Alamo. At the suggestion of my Aunt Edna, my parents named me after Colonel Travis, the commander of the Alamo.

In Texas History Class in Plainview I chose the Alamo for my school project. I researched the history of the Alamo and built a model of it out of sugar cubes. After I got my model back from the school, I ate it. I guess you could say I've got the Alamo in my blood.

---

[2] Colonel William Barrett Travis, as cited by George A. McAlister, *Alamo: The Price of Freedom* (San Antonio, Texas: Docutex, Inc., 1988), 178.

Music added to my Alamo addiction. My mother's friend in Floydada, Betty Batty, had a record with Marty Robbins' song, "Siege of the Alamo." While visiting in Betty's home, I listened to that song on her record player many times.

Walt Disney's version of Davy Crockett, played by San Angelo native Fess Parker, had already made me Alamo crazy even before I took Texas History. When my great aunt Treasure Wilson took me to San Antonio to see the Alamo in person, my imagination went wild with images of battle and heroism.

Even John Wayne contributed to my Alamo addiction when I saw his movie, *The Alamo*, in Plainview at the Twin-Vue Drive-In Theater. Then Wayne helped me link up with another symbol of freedom and patriotism – the Green Berets. Although critics have condemned the movie, *The Green Berets*, as pro-Vietnam War propaganda, I found it inspiring. I still view it as an embodiment of the American ideals of patriotism and the unending fight for freedom – including the freedom of oppressed peoples in other parts of the world.

The movie *The Green Berets* inspired me to read Robin Moore's best selling book by the same name, and Barry Sadler's song, "Ballad of the Green Berets," reinforced my admiration for America's Army Special Forces. The men of the Green Beret brought together the nobility of American patriotism and the excitement of parachuting since they all wore the coveted silver wings of a paratrooper.

One of my friends in Plainview, Gary Cook, joined the Army and succeeded in winning the right to wear the Green Beret. I took great pride in having a friend who had accomplished such a feat, and I viewed him as an American patriot.

Although some patriotic Americans in Plainview never served in the military, I knew of others who had. My friend Randy Morton served his country in both the Army and the Navy. Eldon Box of Plainview served as an Army helicopter door gunner in Vietnam. Steve Seigler made my list of Plainview patriots, and I'll say more about him later.

I didn't know Jimmy Awalt, but I knew his brother, Roger, who graduated with me from Plainview High School in the Class of 1970. Jimmy died in the Vietnam War before our graduation, and Roger felt his loss deeply. Roger himself died in an accident shortly after our high school graduation.

Other men from Plainview had died in Vietnam also, and I felt proud of every one of them and felt that we should not view their deaths as meaningless. As patriots who paid the ultimate price for freedom, they deserve better.

Wanting to Write

My growing desire to write influenced my decision to join the Army. I felt that a good writer needed to experience life at its best and worst, so going to war, in my mind, would help make me a better writer.

During high school in Plainview I ordered a correspondence course for writers. Although I never completed the course, my instructors urged me to start a diary or journal. Much of what you read in this book comes from my journal.

Enlistment

So, patriotism and parachutes and a desire to write contributed to my decision to join the U. S. Army and to volunteer for Vietnam.

My friend Martin Green chose to enlist with me on the Buddy Plan, and that decision allowed us to go through Basic Combat Training together.

At that time you could enlist with a guarantee of some particular job or school, so I enlisted with the guarantee of Airborne School. I didn't know until later that anybody in the Army could volunteer for Jump School and that I could have used my guarantee to secure the kind of job I wanted. I would regret that mistake.

Unlike more thoughtful sons and daughters, I did not consult with my parents before joining the Army. A vocational college in Amarillo had accepted me into their Auto Mechanics program, but going into the Army seemed more exciting and appealed to my hunger for adventure.

I'll never forget the look on Mother's face when I told her what I'd done. I walked into the house and said, "Well, I've found me a job." As expected, she wanted to know more about this new job, so I said, "I've gotten a job working for my rich Uncle Sam."

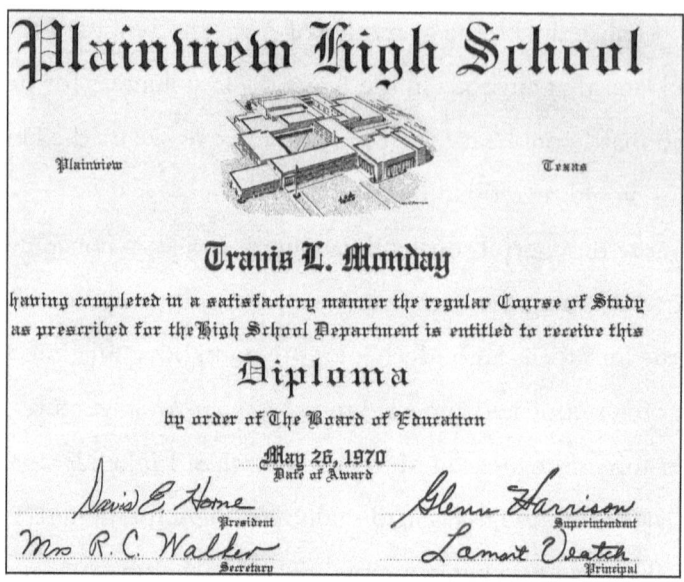

Figure 12 The author's high school diploma from Plainview High School in Plainview, Texas.

Figure 13 Travis Monday with his mother, Wilma, on the day of his graduation from Plainview High School (Author's collection; May 26, 1970).

Figure 14 W. B. Monday, Sr., the author's grandfather (right), on a horse. He received the news that World War I had ended while riding a horse to an Army induction center (Author's collection).

Figure 15 W. B. Monday, Sr., spent most of his adult life as a barber. Many of those years were spent cutting hair in Plainview, Texas (Author's collection).

Figure 16 The author's father, W. B. Monday, Jr. (far right), with his brother and sister, Joe and Juanita (Author's collection).

Figure 17 W. B. Monday, Jr. (left), with his son, Derrell Monday, and his brother, Joe Monday (Author's collection).

Figure 18 W. B. Monday, Jr. (back left) with his mother, Gladys (front left), his sister Juanita, and his brother Joe (Author's collection).

Figure 19 The USS Forrestal on which Joe Monday served during the Vietnam War (U. S. Navy photo).

Figure 20 The author's uncle L. J. Williams (left) with an unidentified sailor. L. J. saw action in the Pacific Theater during World War II (Author's collection).

Figure 21 The USS Alpine destroyer transport on which L. J. Williams served. Japanese kamikaze planes crashed into the ship twice, but it survived both attacks (Author's collection).

Parachutes and Patriotism

Figure 22 Travis Monday (far right) with his brother, Derrell, and his sister, Teressa, in Plainview, Texas (Author's collection).

Figure 23 The author, Travis Monday, during his senior year at Plainview High School in Plainview, Texas (Author's collection).

Basic Combat Training

> A member of your family recently reported to Fort Ord where he is now undertaking basic training. Alongside many other young Americans, he is discharging the responsibility which each of us shares for maintaining the National defense and insuring our preparedness to meet any emergency which may arise.
>
> --Major General Phillip B. Davidson, Jr.

> Early to bed, early to rise.
> Trainee wouldn't be here if he was wise.
>
> --Travis Monday

During World War II American soldiers heading for the west coast usually traveled in trains. While still a boy I rode a train from Lubbock, Texas, to Los Angeles, California. As an adult the Army flew me in a jet airliner from Amarillo, Texas, to an airport in the vicinity of Fort Ord, California.

Since I traveled to California in July, I did not think I needed a coat, but I soon found out that, unlike the part of Texas where I grew up, some parts of California get cold even in the summer. In a letter to Mother dated July 29, 1970, I wrote, "Well, here I am at beautiful sunny California

– don't you believe it! I've only seen the sun twice and almost froze to death until they issued me a field jacket."

Martin and I, along with two other Texans, had made the flight from Amarillo. I had not flown before, so in my first letter home I wrote, "Man that flying is wild."

Since I planned to become a paratrooper, I needed to like flying.

Figure 24 Travis Monday in the push up position at Fort Ord, California, with an M-16 rifle on top of his hands to keep it clean (Author's collection; Fall, 1970).

Fort Ord

Fort Ord got its name from Major General Edward Cresap Ord, who served as a lieutenant with Fremont's Army during California's early history.

In spite of my complaints about cold weather in July, I loved the scenery around Fort Ord, which sat on the Monterey Peninsula about 115 miles south of San Francisco. Having grown up on the prairies of West

Texas, I especially enjoyed looking out of the window of our barracks at beautiful Monterey Bay.

Inprocessing

Before assigning us to our Basic Training units, the Army put us through a series of activities known as "Inprocessing" in an area called "The Reception Center."

Figure 25 Army trainees arriving at Fort Ord, California (U. S. Army photo).

In order to help preserve my memories of Basic Training, I began writing a poem called, "The Ballad of the Basic Combat Trainee." Throughout this chapter I'll share bits and pieces of it. Here's an excerpt about Inprocessing:

>He came from almost anywhere –
>maybe from here, maybe from there.
>He may have enlisted or have been drafted,
>but either way he was bound to feel shafted.
>
>At the Reception Center he lost his hair;
>for some that was just too much to bear.
>When his uniform he finally received,
>of his civilian clothes he was quickly relieved.

> He learned the hard way about taking shots
> as his arm became covered with little red dots.
> Of getting him healthy this was a part,
> but he felt he deserved a Purple Heart.

I'm quite aware that this attempt at poetry by an eighteen-year-old trainee is no literary work of art, but perhaps it conveys a bit of reality in a somewhat humorous manner.

Since Army barbers cut my hair before I received a cap, I suffered severe sunburn on my almost-bald head.

After Inprocessing, our Buddy-Plan approach to enlisting got Martin and me assigned to the same Basic Training unit, Company H, Battalion 2, Brigade 1, shortened for everyday use to "H-2-1."

Basic Combat Training

> Finally he left the Reception Center
> and Basic Training he did enter.
> For eight weeks he'd have to stay.
> As it began he started to pray.

The Army used Basic Training to turn civilians into soldiers. Since all soldiers of all different job descriptions might face combat situations, Basic Training included instruction in basic combat skills.

At that point in my Army experience, I strove to excel in all things. I intended to become an outstanding soldier and to eventually make it into the Specials Forces as a Green Beret. In the military a person with that sort of attitude gets labeled "gung ho," and that label fit me well.

My good friend, Martin, shared my enthusiasm and also excelled in his training. As Texans we expected ourselves to outdo everyone else.

Drill Sergeants or Drill Instructors judged our performance. We referred to them as "D.I.s."

Drill Instructors

> "Trainee" became his new name,
> but the D.I.'s label was not the same.
> To the D.I. he was a stupid fool
> and strict discipline was the only rule.
>
> A soldier out the Trainee he'd make,
> but his methods were too much to take.
> Seeing the D.I. caused the Trainee to shake.
> Trainee, oh Trainee, did you make a mistake?

I didn't mention it in the poem, but we all had white tags on our shirts, and you'll never guess what they called them – "maggot tags!" Until we completed Basic Training, we were low-life maggots, and the D.I.s reminded us often.

Figure 26 Martin E. Green of Plainview, Texas, at Fort Ord, California. Martin joined the Army with the author on what was called the "Buddy Plan" (Photo by author; Fall, 1970).

Actually the D.I.s didn't scare me. In a letter to Mother dated August 6, 1970, I wrote, "The big bad mean Drill Sergeants keep scaring everybody to death with their threats and yelling. So far it hasn't bothered me at all."

After telling Mother that I liked most of the D.I.s and that I thought they were cool, I added, "You always see in the movies about how mean they are. Well, they act like it, but that's all it is – an act. When you learn this, it soon becomes no sweat."

Although Martin and I thrived in the context of Basic Training, some of our fellow trainees didn't handle it well. In the same letter I wrote, "We got some people here who have hated it from the first. One went AWOL (absent without leave) and another cut his wrist with a razor blade."

Figure 27 An inside look at the Army barracks at Fort Ord, California (U. S. Army photo).

Marching

"Yes sir! No sir!" – that's how you talk,
and wherever you go you always walk.
Lead with your left when starting to march.
And make sure your clothes have lots of starch.

Some of my friends in the Plainview High School Band had told me that they enjoyed marching. In Basic Training I enjoyed it too. Singing cadence as we marched made marching both fun and funny. Although I didn't understand all the psychology behind it, the songs helped condition us for war.

For example, I remember singing:

> Two old ladies lyin' in bed,
> one rolled over to the other and said,
> I wanna be an Airborne Ranger.
> I wanna live a life of danger.
> I wanna go to Vietnam.
> I wanna kill some Charlie Cong.

To the tune of "Poison Ivy" we sang:

> Vietnam. Vietnam.
> Late at night while you're sleeping
> Charlie Cong comes a creeping
> all around.
>
> He's pretty as a daisy,
> but look out man he's crazy.
> He'll really do you in
> if you let him catch you sleepin'.

This particular cadence song would have an impact on me in my later life, but I'll save that story for later.

Sometimes we kept in step to this little ditty:

> You had a good job but you LEFT.
> You're RIGHT!
> You had a good girl but you LEFT.
> You're RIGHT!
> Jody was home when you LEFT.
> You're RIGHT!

"Jody" referred to the guy back home who would get your girl while you served your country. The psychology of that sort of song was to build into the developing young soldier an anger that would help prepare him for battle.

As we learned to march, the Drill Instructors taught us to always start with our left foot. Left. Right. Left. Right. If we turned right instead of left while standing or marching, the D.I.s would yell, "Your *military left* you idiots!"

Inspections

> Sweep the barracks; keep them clean,
> 'cause when they dirty the D.I. gets mean.
>
> Make your bunk and keep it tight;
> if it's too loose you'd best take flight.

Figure 28 In Basic Training the trainees had to learn how to make up their bunks the Army way (U. S. Army photo).

Our D.I.s insisted that we keep our bay in the barracks clean and shiny. We swept the floors and buffed them more times than I can remember.

We didn't just shine floors. We shined our brass belt buckles and insignia. And our boots required a lot of attention. We spent many hours learning how to give them a spit shine.

Our D.I.s told us that our bunks had to be so tight that if you dropped a dime on them the dime would bounce. And during inspections the D.I.s reprimanded us for unbuttoned pockets and even loose threads on our uniforms.

Figure 29 Army trainees learning how to salute at Fort Ord, California (U. S. Army photo).

Kitchen Police (K. P.)

> Of course, there's always good 'ol K. P. –
> hell in a kitchen for the poor Trainee.
> Scrub that pan, clean that pot –
> it's dishwater hands the Trainee has got.

In case you can't tell from my poetry, I hated K. P.

First Aid Training

> In First Aid Class you might save a friend
> who got bored, fell asleep, and fell from the stands.

All soldiers need to know first aid, so they taught us the basics.

The comment in the poem about falling asleep during class highlights a frequent dilemma for most of us. Our D.I.s pushed us hard while depriving us of adequate sleep. Staying awake in class often proved difficult.

Physical Training

> Run to the rifle range then run back;
> Strength to keep going the Trainee did lack.
> Yet on he went; he continued to scoot
> for the D.I. behind him had a size 14 boot.

The Army wanted physically fit soldiers, so we exercised frequently and made long runs to and from the rifle ranges, sometimes with full packs and gear. The soft sand of some of the hills made running extra hard.

Because of my Texas pride, I absolutely refused to drop out of any of our runs, no matter how difficult. Even sickness couldn't stop me.

In a letter to Mother dated August 21, 1970, I wrote:

> Today we had to run to the rifle range (5 miles away) and back wearing full gear and carrying our rifles. I've had a sore throat for six days now and today it got worse because of working up a sweat then standing in the cold wind.

Most of us struggled with sickness during Basic Training, including Martin. Early in September we both wound up in the hospital, where a doctor told me I had strep throat.

Getting Gassed

> We're in this room when the gas does appear.
> After that the word "GAS" causes fear.
> Take off your helmet and put on your mask –
> while coughing and crying it's a difficult task.

I can't remember why, but somehow I missed out on getting gassed, but my fellow trainees told me about the experience so that I could describe it in my poem.

During my time in the Army and later in the Texas Army National Guard, I more than made up for not getting gassed in Basic. I've lost count of the times I got gassed during my years in the military.

Learning to Kill

> Learn to fight, learn to kill –
> Trainee learned how to make blood spill.
> Hand-to-hand combat – it's really rough,
> but better not use it unless you're real tough.
>
> Kill! Kill! – that's the spirit of the bayonet.
> Practice for hours; see how good you can get.

Our D.I.s wanted to turn us into killers. The Army gave them that job and they took it seriously. Somehow they managed to inject some humor into this serious task. For example, they'd tell us, "The spirit of the bayonet is to kill!" Then they'd ask, "Men, what's the spirit of the bayonet?" We'd reply, "The spirit of the bayonet is to kill, Drill Sergeant, to kill!"

The D.I.s then said, "No! No! No! The spirit of the bayonet is *not to kill Drill Sergeants*, but *to kill!*"

Earthquake at Fort Ord

Growing up in West Texas, I knew all about tornadoes, but I had no experience with earthquakes. One day as I stood sweeping the floor in front of the entrance to our bay area, the building began to shake. With our bay on the third floor, the men had to run like crazy to get outside. I barely realized what was happening in time to keep from getting trampled to death as the others ran out of the bay entrance to get to the stairs.

Airborne Aspirations

At one point during our training we had to report to our commanding officer. After I snapped to attention and saluted our CO (commanding officer), he asked me where I learned how to report. I told him that I had asked around. He said that I was the first man to do it right, and then told me to sit down.

The C.O. knew I had volunteered for Airborne School, so he talked with me about it, and then invited a 2nd lieutenant wearing jump wings to join our conversation. By the time I left the CO's office, I was even more fired up about going Airborne. I could hardly wait to earn my wings as an Army paratrooper.

Weapons Training

I've already mentioned bayonet training. We also learned how to throw hand grenades, how to fire a 3.5 Rocket Launcher (better known as a "Bazooka"), M79 Grenade Launcher ("Thumper"), and the M72 LAW (Light Anti-tank Weapon).

Our primary weapon consisted of the controversial yet devastating assault rifle called the M-16. Many soldiers had problems with them during the earlier days of the Vietnam War, but by the time I qualified on an M-16A1 most of the problems had been resolved.

My father, W. B. Monday, Jr., taught me to shoot at an early age. I still remember firing his single-shot bolt action 22 caliber rifle while still in the first grade in Hereford, Texas.

I never liked the sights on the M-16, but I managed to fire expert on our first day of qualification. During our night-firing exercises I did not do as well. Out of a possible ranking of expert, sharpshooter, or marksman, I left Basic Training as a sharpshooter.

Infiltration Course

The Army used the Infiltration Course to give us a preview of actual combat. No one shot at us, but live rounds cut through the air above us as we crawled on the ground through barbed wire and around various kinds of obstacles.

Numerous explosions made the experience even more realistic.

We'd all heard stories of trainees standing up and getting cut in half by machine gun fire. I don't know if that actually happened, but I stayed as low and as flat as possible throughout the exercise.

Graduation from Basic Training

Martin and I graduated from Basic Combat Training on Friday, September 25, 1970. In my last letter home from Basic Training, dated September 22, 1970, I wrote, "I will be glad to leave Fort Ord as I am restless and ready to move on to new adventures and new faces."

Figure 30 Travis Monday (front center) and Martin Green (back center) during a break at Fort Ord, California (Author's collection; Fall, 1970).

Figure 31 The author (right) practices hand-to-hand combat with another trainee (Author's collection; Fall, 1970).

Basic Combat Training 49

Figure 32 The Army barracks building at Fort Ord in which the author lived during Basic Training (Photo by author; Fall, 1970).

Figure 33 Private Travis Monday's graduation photo from Basic Training at Fort Ord, California (Author's collection; Fall, 1970).

Lost-in-the-Woods Leadership

Figure 34 The author attended this Leadership Academy at Fort Leonard, Missouri, after Basic Training (Photo by author; October, 1970).

When I left Fort Ord, California, my friend Martin Green remained there for Field Radio School. I arrived at Fort Leonard Wood, Missouri, on October 10, 1970.

Fort Leonard Wood

In 1940 the U. S. Army established Fort Leonard Wood in Pulaski County, Missouri, as a Basic Training Center. The base got its name from Medal-of-Honor winner Major General Leonard Wood.

Leadership Academy

Shortly after arriving at Fort Leonard Wood, I volunteered for a two-week Leadership Preparation Course (LPC) designed to help prepare class leaders for Advanced Individual Training (AIT).

In a letter home dated October 13, 1970, I explained, "This two week school is supposed to be real strict. We have to have highly starched uniforms every day and extremely well-shined boots. We have to set an example as leaders."

Taking the Leadership Preparation Course meant that I'd probably be a platoon leader or squad leader in AIT. What motivated me to volunteer for LPC? The possibility of promotion and the probability of getting out of K. P.

Back at Fort Ord

While at the Leadership Academy at Fort Leonard Wood, I learned that Martin Green had signed up for LPC back at Fort Ord. In a letter dated October 19, 1970, I wrote, "Glad to hear that Clik (Martin's nickname) is in LPC too. That means neither of us will have to pull K. P."

Martin's Field Radio School would have to wait until he completed LPC.

Lost in the Woods

No one likes to gripe more than a soldier, and we did a lot of griping at Fort Leonard Wood. Sometimes soldiers get rather creative with their griping. Soon after my arrival at Fort Leonard Wood, Missouri, I began hearing other soldiers call it, "Fort Lost-in-the-Woods, Misery." That's where I got the title for this chapter about the Leadership Academy – "Lost-in-the-Woods Leadership."

Since LPC required us to adhere to strict discipline and leadership by example, we blew off steam by kidding around. One of my favorite photos from LPC shows some of us in the barracks in our underwear wearing reflective road gear. Anyone looking at that photo might want to say, "If these are our future leaders, then God help us!"

Figure 35 The author (back right) with Edward Arnold (back left) and James Robb sporting reflective road guard gear (Author's collection; October, 1970).

James J. Robb

One of the men in that photo of us clowning around is James J. Robb of Michigan. We befriended one another during LPC, and our friendship would develop further in AIT. He became my best friend at Fort Leonard Wood.

My list of friends at LPC also included Ronald C. Rucker, Edward L. Arnold, and Terrance D. Hutchings, along with a few others.

My First Promotion

As I had hoped, graduating from LPC resulted in my first promotion as a soldier in the U. S. Army. The Army promoted me to Private E-2 on October 31, 1970.

My promotion meant more money and higher status. Lost-in-the-Woods, Misery didn't seem so miserable after all.

Figure 36 James Robb (left) with Travis Monday at the Leadership Academy (Author's collection; October, 1970).

Figure 37 Travis Monday gives Private Currie a lift at the Leadership Academy at Fort Leonard Wood, Missouri (Author's collection; October, 1970).

Airborne Mechanic?

> Engineer, engineer running down the road
> Running so fast makes the others look old
> We're running hard and we're running long
> Still singing another stupid song
> Build a road or cut down a tree
> Or dig some graves for the Infantry.
> Working hard and working all day
> Knocking down anything that gets in the way.
>
> --Army Engineer Cadence Song

I've already mentioned how soldiers like to gripe. I think I'll do a little griping right now. My Army recruiter misled me. I wonder how many other veterans feel the same way. My recruiter allowed me to think that the guarantee of Airborne School included the guarantee of serving in the infantry. I had no way of knowing that cooks, clerks, and others also could volunteer for Jump School and that the Army could give me any job it wanted in spite of my guarantee.

When I joined the Army I knew little about it. My recruiter knew I intended to go beyond Airborne School into Special Forces. He also knew that anybody who could pass the physical fitness test for Airborne School could volunteer and had no need of an enlistment guarantee.

Since I wanted into the infantry, I should have enlisted with the guarantee of Infantry School. Then I could have volunteered for Airborne

School. That approach to enlistment would have put me in a better position to enter Special Forces training or to sign up for Ranger School.

Military Occupational Specialty (MOS)

The Army gives all of its soldiers a job or military occupational specialty (MOS). During Basic Training, the Army tested me to find out what kind of job best suited me. Thanks to Cleo Savage's excellent teaching in Auto Mechanics at Plainview High School, I scored high on those portions of my tests related to mechanical ability.

Along with giving those tests, the Army also asked me what job I wanted, and I requested the infantry. At a time when most folks tried to avoid the infantry, I tried to get into it. At the same time, I also volunteered for Vietnam.

By the time I left Fort Ord, I already knew that the Army had decided to send me to Engineer Equipment Repairman School at Fort Leonard Wood. My MOS would be 62B10 – Heavy Equipment Repairman. I was not a happy camper because I wanted Infantry School.

Army Engineers

The U. S. Army Engineers have a proud tradition of service both in times of war and in times of peace. To my fellow veterans who served in the Army Engineers, I want you to know that I'm proud to have served in two different engineer units even though I had asked for the infantry.

Advanced Individual Training (AIT)

After Basic Combat Training, most soldiers in the U. S. Army entered Advanced Individual Training (AIT) in order to train for their primary MOS. Martin Green and I both started AIT later than most soldiers just finishing Basic so that we first could take the Army's Leadership Preparation Course (LPC).

AIT for Martin meant going to the Field Radio School at Fort Ord. For me it meant going through the Engineer Equipment Repairman Course at Fort Leonard Wood. For AIT the Army assigned me to Company A, 3rd Battalion, 4th AIT Brigade, USATC Engineers.

Figure 38 Members of the author's Heavy Equipment Repairman Class get acquainted with an Army bulldozer (Photo by author; Winter, 1970-1971).

AIT Leadership

In a letter dated November 8, 1970, I wrote, "I went to a Leadership Academy when I got here and came out of it as assistant platoon leader. I start AIT tomorrow."

James Robb and I, both graduates of LPC, became the class leaders for Co. A, 3rd Bn., 4th AIT Bde. Our unit generally went by the designation,

"A-3-4, Class 10." Robb got the job of class leader and I worked with him as assistant class leader.

No K. P., but . . .

As Robb and I had hoped, our leadership positions in AIT got us out of K. P. and out of some other details, but they also gave us a good taste of the burden of leadership. Both of us faced the unpleasant task of choosing people for various details, including K. P., so we had people mad at us all the time.

Figure 39 More of the heavy equipment at Fort Leonard Wood, Missouri (Photo by author; Winter 1970-1971).

Regular Army versus Army National Guard & Reserves

Another cause of headaches for Robb and me consisted of animosity between the Regular Army soldiers and the soldiers in the Army National Guard. Robb and I also had a hard time getting some of the National

Guard troops to do their share of the work. I did not know at that time that I, too, would one day serve in the Army National Guard.

We also had some Army Reserve troops in our company who had some of the same tendencies as the National Guard troops. Members of both the National Guard and the Army Reserves were often called "Weekend Warriors."

In truth we had some deadbeats in the Regular Army, the Army National Guard, and the Army Reserves. We also had some fine soldiers in all of these groups.

Bunk Bed Blues

Since we served as class leaders, our fellow soldiers sometimes gave Robb and me a hard time. I remember having a trash can full of water dumped on us as we entered our barracks, but that's nothing compared to what they did to us one night.

When Robb and I returned to the barracks after seeing a movie, we discovered that our bunk beds had mysteriously disappeared. We soon discovered that the men in our company had completely disassembled our bunks and had scattered the pieces throughout the building. It took us most of the night to find all the pieces and reassemble our bunks.

Too Cold to Cope

Growing up in the panhandle of Texas, I had seen plenty of snow and had even experienced a blizzard or two, but the cold I encountered at Fort Leonard Wood, Missouri, seemed worse than anything I had experienced elsewhere.

In a letter dated November 24, 1970, I said, "You think it's been cold there, you should've been here yesterday. It was 15 degrees below zero with high winds."

Having grown up in Michigan, Robb handled the cold better than me.

Airborne Aspirations Continued

Even though I had already volunteered for Airborne School and had even enlisted with a guarantee for that school, I still had to sign an "Application for Airborne Training" at Fort Leonard Wood. I signed it on November 14, 1970.

The form, DA FORM 2496, contained this statement:

> I volunteer to perform frequent aircraft flights, parachute jumps, and to participate in realistic combat training while securing Airborne Training, and/or performing Airborne duty for a period of not less than one year upon satisfactory completion of the prescribed course.

Along with signing this application form, I also had to take an "Airborne Physical Training Test" (AR 611-7). The test required me to do six chin-ups, twenty sit-ups, twenty-two push ups, eighty knee benders (in 2 minutes or less), and run a mile in under eight and a half minutes. I easily met these qualifications but found the task rather unpleasant because of snow and ice and cold weather.

As I thought of going to Airborne School, I decided that I did not want to go without my friends, so I tried to talk some of them into going with me. In spite of the fact that he suffered from a fear of heights, James Robb agreed to join me in my great adventure. He, too, easily passed the Airborne Physical Training Test.

Heavy Equipment

At Plainview High School in Cleo Savage's Auto Mechanics Class, I had learned primarily about working on gasoline engines in cars and trucks. At Fort Leonard Wood's Heavy Equipment Repairman School they focused more on diesel engines.

As a mechanic I had to know how to operate the Army's heavy equipment well enough to work on it, so I drove numerous types of heavy equipment. I especially enjoyed driving bulldozers and front-end loaders (also referred to as "bucket loaders" and "scoop loaders").

Driving these big machines reminded me of driving a Massy-Ferguson 410 Combine in Kansas one summer while I was fifteen years old. Because of a shortage of drivers, the boss had taken me to Kansas with him even though I had never driven a combine.

One day, as the boss' son sat on a combine with me teaching me how to operate it, I said, "Ya'll sure took a big chance in bringing me up here without knowing for sure that I'd be able to drive one of these things. What if I couldn't learn how?" He replied, "It's a long walk back to Texas." I learned how.

Figure 40 A front-end loader, also called a "scoop loader" and a "bucket loader," at Fort Leonard Wood, Missouri (Photo by author; Winter 1970-1971).

My First Army Leave

After Basic Combat Training at Fort Ord, California, I could have taken my first leave from the Army, but I chose instead to save it for Christmas. I don't remember much about my first leave except that Mother and Glynn wanted to take some pictures and I visited some friends and relatives.

When I had left Plainview to enter the Army, I couldn't wait to get out of town. Somehow, after spending some time in the Army, Plainview didn't seen like such a bad place after all.

Figure 41 Private E-2 Travis Monday back at home in Plainview, Texas, during his first leave from the Army (Author's collection; December, 1970).

Orders for Fort Benning

Soon after returning to Fort Leonard Wood, I received my orders for Fort Benning, Georgia, where I would attend Airborne School. In a letter dated January 4, 1971, I wrote, "Most of my class was stationed in the

States, with one in England, and a few in Germany. I still don't know where I'm going after Airborne."

I graduated from the Army's Engineer Equipment Repairman Course on January 15, 1971.

The Grind of Ground Week

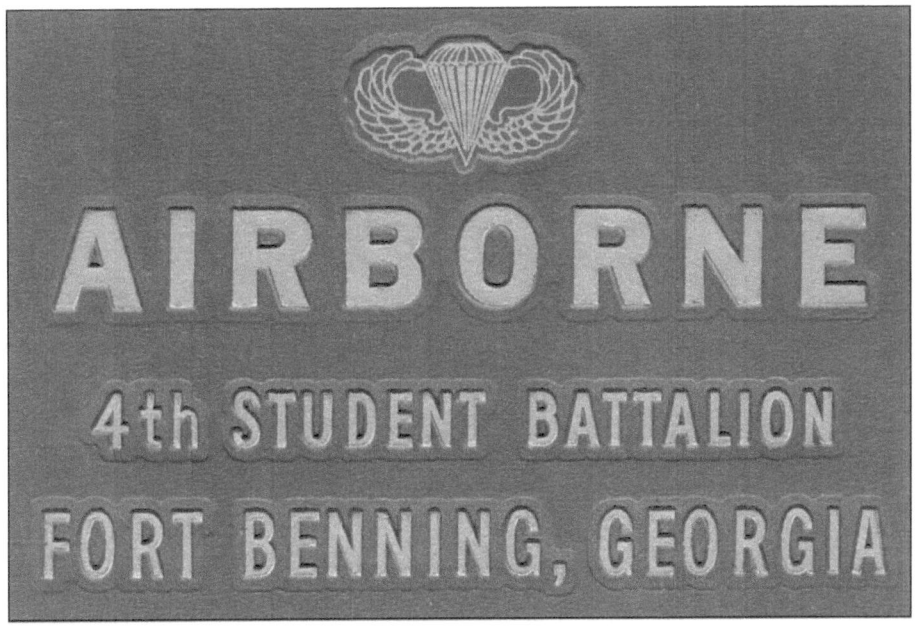

In his book, *Airborne: A Guided Tour of an Airborne Task Force*, Tom Clancy calls his section on Airborne School, "Jump School: Three Weeks at Hell's Gate."[1]

---

[1] Tom Clancy, *Airborne: A Guided Tour of an Airborne Task Force* (New York: Berkley Books, 1997), 63.

While I did not think of Jump School as the entrance into hell, I did expect a challenge. My first letter home from Fort Benning, dated January 18, 1971, included this statement: "From what I've seen and heard, the training here is really rough. I think I'll dig it."

Fort Benning, Georgia

Located southwest of Columbus, Georgia, Fort Benning got its name from Confederate General Henry L. Benning, a soldier from Columbus. Established in 1918, later during World War II it became the home of the U. S. Army's first paratrooper units, including the original Test Platoon. Benning became known as the "Cradle of American Airborne."

Figure 42 Statue of infantryman at Fort Benning, Georgia (Photo by author; Winter, 1971).

Airborne Concepts and Principles

Some historians credit Benjamin Franklin with inventing the concept of Airborne troops. Later Billy Mitchell pushed for the development of

American paratroopers. When the Army got serious about forming its own Airborne forces, it began the process at Fort Benning by forming a Test Platoon.

From the beginning, the American Army approach to Airborne training and service included the concept of voluntary participation. That approach still held true when I joined the Airborne and it continues to this day. As Clancy explains, "Nobody in the U. S. Army can be ordered to go to jump school, and everyone who does is a volunteer."[2]

By the time I arrived at Fort Benning, more than a million student jumps had been made there.

Airborne Class 24

The Army assigned me to Class 24, which included the 43rd and 47th Companies of the 4th Student Battalion, The Student Brigade (Airborne). Since the Army put me in the 47th Company, my company commander was Captain Thomas Y. Hiter. Second Lieutenant Hanley W. Clifford served as our executive officer, and First Sergeant James Evans as our top NCO (non-commissioned officer).

Martin Green at Fort Benning

Martin Green, who had joined the Army with me on the Buddy Plan, also made it to Fort Benning after AIT. In fact, he started Airborne School one week ahead of me.

While we did not train together in the same cycle or the same class, Martin and I managed to see each other frequently and to go to some movies on weekends.

---

[2] Clancy, 63.

Fort Benning versus Fort Leonard Wood

Fort Benning had a more positive atmosphere than Fort Leonard Wood. Instead of the drudgery I often faced at Leonard Wood, Benning seemed alive with energy and excitement. I felt like I had entered a totally different world.

As for the facilities, both Leonard Wood and Benning had old wooden barracks, unlike the newer steel and concrete barracks of Fort Ord.

The similarity of housing did not carry over into the food. During AIT I hated the food the Army fed me, but at Fort Benning the food was great. To me almost everything about Fort Benning seemed characterized by quality or excellence.

Figure 43 Martin Green (left) and Travis Monday at Fort Benning, Georgia (Winter, 1971).

Ground Week

I'm not sure about all those who went before me, but the Basic Airborne Course (BAC) lasted for three weeks during my time in it. They called week one Ground Week, week two Tower Week, and week three Jump Week.

Ground Week focused on learning some basic concepts, skills, and commands. The physical training during Ground Week helped prepare us for the final two weeks and for making parachute jumps and landings without serious injury.

Ground Week also served to introduce Airborne students to the history, traditions, and enthusiastic spirit of Airborne.

Although I don't have exact figures and am working strictly by memory, I believe our class contained over four hundred students at the beginning of Ground Week.

The Black Hats at Fort Benning

The Black Hats who led us through the Airborne Course got their names from the black baseball-style caps they wore. You might say that they were the D.I.s (Drill Instructors) of Jump School. My Airborne School Class Book says of the Black Hats: "95% of the instruction is presented by highly qualified noncommissioned officers, all of who are combat veterans and have experience in Airborne units."[3]

Although they sometimes gave me and my fellow Airborne students a hard time, I had the utmost respect for the Black Hats. They were top-of-the-line – the best in the world.

---

[3] *Airborne: 4th Student Battalion* (Class Book) (Fort Benning, Georgia: Winter, 1971), 2.

By the way, even the officers in Jump School submitted to the leadership and instruction of the Black Hats, and I'm certain that the Black Hats got a great deal of pleasure out of that since all of them were NCOs.

Clancy says of these instructors: "The Black Hats are the tribal elders of the paratroopers, and the keepers of their traditions."[4]

Airborne Discipline and Expectations

Those Black Hats taught us about Airborne discipline and expectations. For example, we learned that there is no such thing as walking on Airborne grass. We ran everywhere we went except when slowing down just long enough to salute an officer. Saluting during Airborne School differed from what we'd learned before. If we saluted an officer, we'd say, "Airborne! Sir!" The officer would then return our salute and say, "All the Way!"

Part of the discipline of Airborne included learning to take harassment. For example, one day during a brief break, a Black Hat approached me and looked at my name tag, which contained my last name, "Monday." He asked, "What is your name, soldier?" "Monday, Sergeant!" He then looked at me and yelled, "You think you're smart, don't you? Get down and give me ten (ten push ups)!"

Airborne Physical Training

While I'm on the subject of push ups, we also did lots of pull-ups and sit-ups, but the heart and soul of Airborne P.T. (physical training) consisted of running. Every morning we ran before breakfast. During the

---

[4] Clancy, 63.

first week we started with only a couple of miles every morning. I think we ran over three miles on the last morning of Ground Week.

These morning runs resulted in numerous disqualifications from Jump School. You either made the runs without dropping out or you did not finish the Airborne Course. By the time I graduated from Jump School, our class of over four hundred students had dwindled down to about two hundred and sixty. Most of those who didn't make it left during the grind of Ground Week, and most of them got disqualified for dropping out of our morning runs.

Parachute Landing Falls

The Army did not want us to make stand-up landings during our jumps as paratroopers, so our instructors taught us how to fall instead. We called these intentional falls Parachute Landing Falls or PLFs, and we spent a lot of time practicing PLFs during Ground Week. We practiced by jumping off of platforms of different heights, starting first with 2-foot platforms and then moving up to the 4-foot platforms.

In order to perform successful PLFs, we had to learn the five points of contact – places on our bodies that should hit the ground in order to absorb the impact without injuring us.

C-130 Mock Exits

During Ground Week the Black Hats paired our PLF training with instruction on how to exit an aircraft in flight. One of the training aids they used consisted of a C-130 Mock Exit Assembly. This teaching tool, painted gray as I remember it, roughly simulated a small portion of a C-130 fuselage without the skin. The designers sought to make the openings or doors similar to the ones in a real C-130.

We would line up behind these simulated aircraft doors and practice jumping out. After standing in the door with our hands on each side of us against the outer frame of the door, we'd jump out and land in a small pit.

As we exited the mock door, we'd assume a tight body position with our hands on each side of our reserve parachutes and count, "One thousand, two thousand, three thousand, four thousand," and then we'd reach up and grab our imaginary risers while also looking up to check our imaginary canopies.

"Hit It!"

In order to reinforce our learning of the Army's approach to exiting an aircraft, the Black Hats employed an exercise called, "Hit It!" You never knew when a Black Hat might suddenly shout, "Hit it!" When we heard that command, we immediately jumped about six inches into the air, assumed a good tight body position, and counted to four in the manner already described. The exercise included looking up to check our canopies.

This training exercise ended with the command "Recover." By the end of Ground Week, we had practiced it so many times that it had become second nature to us.

34 Foot Mock Towers

Another training aid used for teaching us how to exit aircraft in flight was the 34 Foot Mock Tower. Wearing a parachute harness that included a reserve parachute, we'd climb several flights of stairs to the top of the towers, where we'd jump out of a simulated aircraft door. As with the C-130 Mock Exit Assembly, we'd assume a tight body position, with our hands placed firmly on each side of our reserve parachute packs, and count to four.

At some point in this process we'd experience a sudden jerk as our harnesses, connected to a metal cable overhead, ran out of slack and stopped our fall. This jerking sensation helped prepare us for the opening shock of a real parachute.

Figure 44 34 Foot Mock Towers at Fort Benning, Georgia. Jumping from these towers resulted in a trolley ride down steel cables after experiencing a jerking sensation designed to simulate the opening shock of a parachute (Photo by author; Winter, 1971).

After experiencing this jerking sensation, we took a little ride – sometimes called a "trolley ride" -- on a pulley-like assembly that rolled down the cable toward a mound located near the towers. Some of our fellow Airborne students stood on the mound to catch us as we spread out our legs and arms so they'd have something to grab to stop us.

Five Basic Jump Techniques

To our training on how to exit aircraft and on performing PLFs, the Black Hats added instruction on the Five Basic Jump Techniques. These techniques consisted of:

> (1) Control of the jumper inside the aircraft prior to jumping.
> (2) Control of the jumper's body from the door of the aircraft until he receives the opening shock.
> (3) Control of parachute during descent.
> (4) Making contact with the ground (PLF).
> (5) Control of the parachute once the jumper is on the ground.[5]

You probably noticed that these jump techniques focus primarily on the idea of *control*. Safe parachute jumping requires concentration and control.

Nine Jump Commands

While jumpers ride in an aircraft toward their designated DZ (Drop Zone), a man in charge of the jump known as the Jumpmaster guides them through a series of tasks by giving them a series of commands.

Following is a description of those commands as presented in my Airborne Class Book and as explained from the perspective of an Airborne student:

> I learned the commands: "get ready," "outbound personnel stand up," "Inboard personnel stand up," "hook up," "check static lines," "check equipment," "sound off for equipment check," "stand in the door" and "go." The technique is taught from a mockup of a C-130 aircraft.[6]

---

[5] *Airborne: 4th Student Battalion* (Class Book), 2.

[6] Ibid., 2.

Ground Week Completed

Clancy indicates that the survivors of Ground Week "spend the coming weekend sleeping and healing from any minor injuries that they might have acquired during the week."[7]

In a letter home I wrote, "I made it through Ground Week without any trouble."

---

[7] Clancy, 69.

Figure 45 A paratrooper-in-training jumps from a 34 Foot Mock Tower at Fort Benning, Georgia (U. S. Army photo).

Those Terrific Towers

Figure 46 Airborne students about to drop from the 250 Foot Towers at Fort Benning, Georgia (U. S. Army photo).

They call it, "The Texas Chute-Out." In Arlington, Texas, at the amusement park called Six Flags Over Texas, a tall tower stretches into the sky with horizontal arms at the top reaching out in multiple directions. The ride carries people to the top then lets them down with a cable-connected parachute overhead.

Although the tower at Six Flags Over Texas reminds me of the 250 Foot Towers at Fort Benning, Georgia, the cables or wires that assure a safe descent ruined the ride for me. The amusement park ride just doesn't cut it when compared with the towers at Fort Benning.

250 Foot Towers

Because it's an older black and white film, many people today haven't seen the movie starring Dean Martin and Jerry Lewis called *Jumping Jacks*. One of my favorite scenes shows Jerry Lewis training on the towers at Fort Benning. It makes me laugh every time I see it.

While living in Colorado City, Texas, I put together a video tape of my military experiences, and in the process I did some experimenting. Turning off the sound to the tower scene in *Jumping Jacks*, I watched it while playing Buddy Holly's hit song, "That'll Be the Day." Sure worked for me.

Figure 47 The 250 Foot Towers at Fort Benning, Georgia (Photo by author; Winter, 1971).

At the New York World Fair in 1939, visitors could ride up tall towers and then come down at the bottom of a parachute. After the early leaders of the American Airborne Test Platoon saw these towers, they tried them out as training aids for their student paratroopers. Soon thereafter, they built four towers at Fort Benning, and they've used them there through all of these years of American Airborne history. One of the towers blew over in a gale, but the other three towers continue in use today.

As you've probably figured out, Week Two of Airborne School gets its name from the 250 Foot Free Towers.

More P.T.

The inclusion of training on the 250 Foot Free Towers did not mean an end to physical training. We still had to run on Airborne grass, and we still had our morning runs before breakfast. In fact, the length of the runs increased.

Figure 48 Airborne students on one of their daily runs at Fort Benning (U. S. Army photo).

And, of course, we still did countless push ups, sit-ups, and pull-ups.

I remember a push up contest staged by the Black Hats. They enlisted a volunteer from the Army and a volunteer from the Marines, and let each one do as many push ups as possible. The Army volunteer won.

Although the Army won the push up contest, I seem to remember that a smaller percentage of the Marines dropped out of Airborne School than Army soldiers.

Suspended Agony

The most painful experience for me at Jump School consisted of the training I endured on a device known as the Suspended Harness. The straps that went between our legs and carried most of our weight, even when properly placed, produced terrible pain.

Because of the pain of training in this particular harness assembly, Airborne students changed the name from "Suspended Harness" to "Suspended Agony." The latter name fits perfectly.

Swing Landing Training

Along with the Suspended Harness we trained on another harness-type device known as the Swing Landing Trainer. The purpose of the Swing Landing Trainer was to give us practice in learning how to perform PLFs from various directions since our drift in descent and our body position could vary greatly.

For example, if I landed while drifting to my left, I'd perform a left PLF. But if I landed while drifting left and forward, I'd perform a left front PLF. From these examples you can see the many possibilities.

Wind Machine

As Army parachutists we had to consider the wind whenever we jumped. The wind influenced the direction of our drift, the type of PLFs we performed, and how hard we hit the ground. Even a perfect PLF cannot prevent injuries or death if the wind is blowing too hard. I've read about whole teams of expert jumpers dying because of high winds.

And even after a safe landing the wind can create problems for a parachutist. The wind can grab a jumper's canopy and drag him to death or leave him severely injured.

Figure 49 Airborne students at Fort Benning learn how to escape from a wind-blown parachute. Notice the large fan used to simulate windy conditions (U. S. Army photo).

Because of this danger the Army parachute harness contains a quick-release mechanism to enables the jumper to release one or both of his riser assemblies in order to collapse the canopy. Our Airborne training included the use of a Wind Machine that looked like an oversized fan. This device enabled us to learn to use the quick-release mechanisms while actually getting dragged across the ground by a wind-filled parachute.

Airborne Cadence Song

Paratroopers sing and shout and make strange noises. As with other military units, Airborne units sing cadence songs while they march.

In the first chapter I shared excerpts from the Airborne classic, "Blood on the Risers." As I prepared to include words from another Airborne classic cadence song, I started searching the internet to see if I could find a copy. Even though many years had passed, I could reproduce the song from memory, but I wanted to find a copy for comparison.

Instead of finding a copy of one version, I found numerous versions, none of which matched my version exactly. I guess most cadence songs exist in various versions, and some versions probably get lost in the "shuffle" – Airborne Shuffle that is!

So I've decided to reproduce the version I learned during my military service. Here it is:

> C-130 rollin' down the strip,
> Airborne Daddy gonna take a little trip.
> Stand up, hook up, shuffle to the door,
> jump right out and count to four.
>
> If my main don't open wide,
> I've got another one by my side.
> If my reserve don't open round,
> I'll be the first one on the ground.
>
> If I die on the ol' drop zone,
> box me up and send me home.
> Pin my wings upon my chest,
> and tell my girl I did my best.

Along with this ending, I learned an alternate ending that goes like this:

> If I die on the ol' drop zone,
> box me up and ship me home.
> Pin my wings upon my chest,
> and bury me in the front leaning rest.

For those of you who don't understand the terminology "front leaning rest," that's the position used for doing push ups. Some shorten it to just "leaning rest," but they used the longer version when I went through Airborne School.

Airborne Chapel

Singing songs about death on the drop zone can motivate a person to think about spiritual realities. Maybe that's why they built an Airborne Chapel at Fort Benning. I don't remember how many times I attended services in the Airborne Chapel, but I do remember the chaplain — they called him "Jumpin' Jesus."

What most impressed me about Jumpin' Jesus was his jumping. He made a practice of making the first jump with every class of Airborne students. No telling how many jumps that chaplain made.

Figure 50 The Airborne Chapel at Fort Benning, Georgia (U. S. Army photo).

If any of you readers know the real name of the Airborne chaplain at Fort Benning in the winter of 1971, I'd like to have it. He didn't make it into my Airborne Class Book.

Parachute Riggers

An Airborne chaplain could jump with us and pray for us, but we also needed someone to pack our parachutes. The name for these 'chute folders is "rigger."

I don't know if it's true now, but when I went through Airborne School, riggers occasionally had to jump with a parachute they packed, and they never knew which one. No wonder they did such a great job!

Years later, while living and working in Sweetwater, Texas, I met a man who packed parachutes for the WASP (Women Airforce Service Pilots) of World War II.

H. B. Stevens went from selling sewing machines for Singer to packing parachutes at Avenger Field near Sweetwater. One of his parachutes saved the life of WASP Cadet Meredith Rolfe when she fell out of an open-cockpit training aircraft. The Pioneer Parachute Company gave Stevens a plaque with Rolfe's name on it.[1]

Jump Boots

We didn't pack our own parachutes, but we polished our own boots – jump boots! Anyone who knows anything about Army paratroopers knows that we take great pride in our jump boots. I sure liked wearing mine with my dress uniforms rather than those wimpy-looking dress shoes.

This may sound strange, but I seldom jumped in my jump boots. Instead, I kept them polished and looking good while jumping in regular

---

[1] Travis Monday, "WASP, Parachutes, and Riggers," in *Ultimate Museum Musings* (United States of America: Travis Monday, 2007), 233-5.

Army boots. I did make one jump in my jump boots just to make sure the name fit.

Trying the Towers

Now let's get back to those 250 Foot Towers. As Week Two progressed, I anxiously waited for my turn. On February 2, 1971, I wrote in my journal: "Training on the 250 Foot Tower was started today in my class, but not my company. Perhaps I'll get my chance tomorrow."

In the same journal entry I also noted: "Clik (Martin Green) made his first two jumps today. I envy him and look forward to my first jump."

The following day I completed my training on the 34 Foot Tower, but once again I didn't get to try out one of the 250 Foot Towers.

Finally, on February 4, 1971, I got my turn. That night I wrote in my journal: "I finally got to go off the 250 Foot Tower. I really did like it. I feel as though I'm ready to jump now, but unfortunately, the first jump is not scheduled until Monday."

That evening I also wrote: "I have not dropped out of a run and, of course, I'm not about to tomorrow."

Parachutes Burned

On the same night that I made my first drop from a 250 Foot Tower, a fire destroyed over 3,000 parachutes. I don't have much information on the fire, but I wrote in my journal, "It was thought to have been started by lightning."

Tower Week Completed

"My first two weeks of Jump School are now finished," I wrote on February 5, 1971.

As I completed Tower Week, Martin completed Jump School. In my journal I wrote: "Clik made his graduation jump today so he now wears silver wings upon his chest."

Figure 51 One of the 250 Foot Towers in use at Fort Benning, Georgia (U. S. Army photo).

The Joy of Jump Week

Figure 52 The silver wings of the U. S. Army paratrooper.

With two weeks of Airborne School behind me, I waited impatiently for a chance to jump out of a "perfectly good airplane." In a letter home dated February 7, 1971, I wrote: "Tomorrow is the big day. If the weather is good I'll make my first jump. Clik (Martin Green) leaves for Fort Bragg Wednesday, and, of course, has his wings. He sure is proud of them."

Airborne Aircraft

Before I could share Martin's pride by wearing my own set of jump wings, I had to make five jumps from military transport aircraft. We often sang about a "C-130 rollin' down the strip," but I would start my military parachuting adventures by jumping from the older Fairchild C-119 Flying Boxcar. The twin-boomed C-119 had first flown in 1947, and by 1955 production had ceased. U. S. military forces had used C-119s during the Korean War.

After the United States entered the fight in South Vietnam, some C-119s served in a ground support role after their transformation into AC-119 gun ships. During my journey through Jump School, I saw plenty of C-119s.

Along with the C-119s, I also saw C-130s at Fort Benning. Even before my own Jump Week I had seen both of these aircraft flying overhead.

A third aircraft in use at the time, the C-141 Starlifter, didn't drop me or any of my fellow Airborne students during our cycle of training, but I'd later get my opportunity to jump a jet.

Figure 53 A C-130 Hercules on display at Dyess Air Force Base in Abilene, Texas (Photo by author).

Airborne Parachutes

When we loaded onto one of these Airborne aircraft, we'd each carry strapped to our body a T-10 military parachute designed for static line jumps.

By the time I went through Airborne School, the T-10 had passed the test of time. Developed from the earlier T-4, the T-10 sported a 28-foot canopy and included a reserve parachute for use in emergencies.

Jump Week

In order to win my wings, I'd have to make five successful jumps with T-10 parachutes. During Jump Week I expected to make those jumps.

I'm calling this chapter "The Joy of Jump Week," but sometimes frustration blocked the joy, especially the frustration of not jumping.

First Day Frustration

On Monday, February 8, 1971, I felt that frustration. In my journal I wrote, "Unhappily, I didn't get to jump today because of bad weather. I'm supposed to jump twice tomorrow."

Figure 54 Martin Green at Fort Benning (Photo by author; Winter, 1971).

Something else happened that same day to dampen my spirits. My friend Martin Green left Fort Benning for Fort Bragg, North Carolina. The Army had assigned him to the famed 82nd Airborne Division – the All Americans.

Second Day Surprise

Although the frustration of not jumping hit me again the next day, a surprising development forced out the frustration. Most of the soldiers graduating from Airborne School at that time, like Martin Green, went to the 82nd Airborne Division. For that reason I fully expected to rejoin Martin at Fort Bragg, but I clearly remember how that expectation got shattered.

While I sat in the barracks pouting about not getting to jump for the second day in a row, a guy came walking in and asked, "Is your name Monday?"

"Yes it is."

"Well, I just saw your name on the list for Vietnam."

He had my attention. I immediately found out where the assignments had been posted and verified his report. The Army had assigned me to overseas duty in the Republic of South Vietnam.

Of course, I had volunteered for Vietnam, but so had many other soldiers. Ongoing efforts to reduce America's overall troop strength in Vietnam had made my going seem highly unlikely.

That night in my journal I wrote: "I saw my alert orders today. I'm on the list for Vietnam. The four guys who came here from Fort Leonard Wood with me are also going to Vietnam. It will definitely be a good experience but I just hope I don't have to kill anyone."

Tuesday, February 9th, also stands out in my mind because I bought my first pair of jump boots and started polishing them.

Third Day Thrill

After two days of disappointment, jumping twice on Wednesday made my day. In a letter home I said, "It was really great and I loved it. Three more jumps and I'll have my wings. I'm ready to jump now it's so much fun."

Indeed, both jumps went well, but in my jump record I mentioned a slight problem with the second jump: "Good jump with hard landing."

Figure 55 Airborne students complete a training jump at Fort Benning, Georgia (U. S. Army photo).

As novice jumpers, the jumpmasters signaled us when to jump by using individual tap-outs and by shouting, "Go!" Later only the first jumper would get an individual signal, and everyone else would follow him out automatically in a manner known as a "mass exit."

We left the aircraft that day with less weight than on other jumps known as "Equipment Jumps." When we jumped without all of our regular military gear, we called them "Hollywood Jumps."

I made my first two jumps from an altitude of 1250 feet and from C-119s. In spite of my earlier comments about the worn-out condition of the C-119s, in my journal I wrote, "They were very efficient for the job."

In a letter home written that same day, I told Mother about my first two jumps and about Vietnam. Knowing that she would worry about me getting wounded or killed in Vietnam, I assured her, "There's very little going on over there right now and, as a mechanic, I will be relatively safe."

Fourth Day Fulfillment

Figure 56 Airborne students boarding a C-119 Flying Boxcar at Fort Benning, Georgia (U. S. Army photo).

The following day, Thursday, I made two more jumps from C-119s from 1250 feet. The first of these two jumps, another Hollywood, I described in my jump record as "excellent all round."

Figure 57 Airborne students gain control of their parachutes after landing (U. S. Army photo).

After loading up for another jump, a Combat Equipment Jump, we flew back into Alabama and made a mass exit. Leaving the aircraft proved more difficult this time because of the extra weight. Then, as I checked my canopy, I spotted several small holes.

The Black Hats taught us how to judge the size of holes in our canopies so that we'd know whether or not to pull the ripcord on our reserve parachutes. They said, "If the hole is smaller than your helmet, then you probably won't need to pop your reserve." When I studied the holes in my canopy, I decided that they were smaller than my helmet, but there were several of them. A more important criterion for deciding about using our reserves had to do with our rate of descent. If we saw that we were descending considerably faster than the jumpers around us, we should activate them.

Because of the problems created by descending with two canopies, including difficulty with PLFs, I did not want to activate my reserve. So, after discerning that my rate of descent was only slightly faster than that of my fellow jumpers, I decided to ride my T-10 main parachute all the way to the ground.

After preparing to land, I hit the ground like a sack of cement, but landing in mud and water helped cushion the shock of impact. I walked away uninjured.

Before I went to bed that night, I wrote in my journal, "I'm now only one jump away from those beautiful silver wings."

Figure 58 Silver wings of a U. S. Army paratrooper (U. S. Army photo).

Fifth Day Frustration

The fifth day of Week Three, Friday, jerked away the joy of Jump Week. In my journal I described the discouraging developments:

> Today was definitely the most disgusting day since I've been in Airborne. Everyone made their last jump except three plane loads, and I just happened to be in one of them. We were hooked-up and ready to jump, but, due to high winds, we had to land in the C-119. We few had to stand outside while the largest part of our class got their wings. It was a sick feeling.

The frustration of that fifth day of Jump Week worsened as the hope of a Saturday jump fell through due to bad weather, and Monday turned out to be a holiday.

Silver Wings upon *My* Chest!

Finally, on Tuesday, February 16, 1971, I made my qualifying jump – a Hollywood from a C-130 Hercules. In my jump record I wrote, "Perfect all round jump."

Afterwards the remnant of our class held graduation on DZ Fryar, where we all received our wings.

Between Jump School and Leave

Soon after graduating from Airborne School, I moved from the 47th Company to Headquarters Company. Three of my good friends ended up in the same barracks with me: James Robb, Edward Kondo, and Marshall Forshey.

On February 17, I wrote in my journal, "I spent today processing. I got my leave orders and I am to report to Oakland Army Base on 17 March '71."

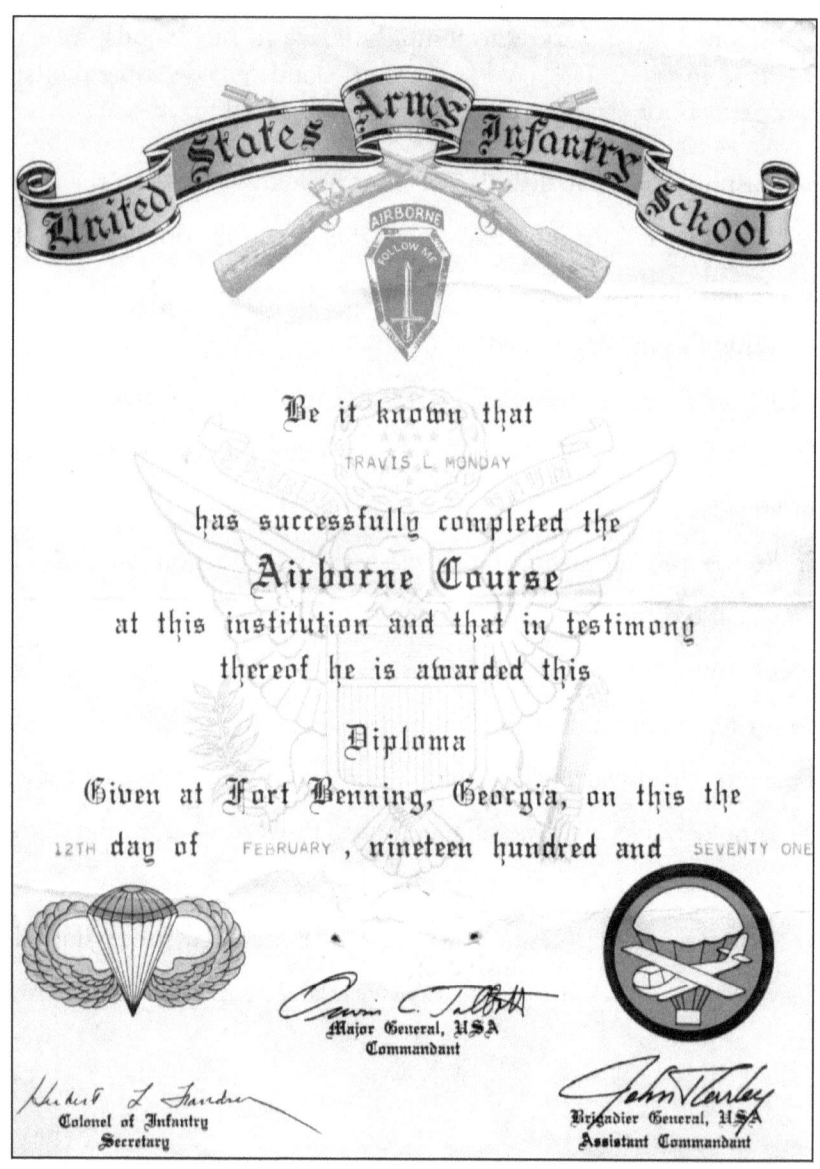

Figure 59 Airborne School diploma of Travis Monday (Author's collection).

America -- Love It *Then* Leave It

During the Vietnam War some patriotic Americans would get upset with complaints and protests against the War. Sometimes, in frustration, they would say in response to these complaints and protests, "America – love it or leave it!"

In my case going home on leave and then going to war meant both loving America *and* leaving it. Loving America included loving my family and friends before leaving them in order to serve my country. In my mind, serving my country meant more than mere political ideology; it meant serving my family and friends in the most meaningful way possible.

Arrival in Amarillo

Three days after graduating from Airborne School, I left Fort Benning, Georgia, to travel home for leave. I arrived in Amarillo, Texas, on February 20, 1971.

Mother met me at the airport in Amarillo, and then we traveled home to Plainview by car. Anytime I went home for leave from the Army, I knew Mother would be there for me. Since I would soon leave for Vietnam, her loving reception meant the world to me.

At some point during my journey, Mother gave me some news that hit hard. Steven Lee Seigler had died in Vietnam about a week before my arrival back in Plainview. I had talked with Steve shortly before I left town to enter the Army and shortly before he left for Vietnam.

Figure 60 Steve Seigler of Plainview, Texas, in Vietnam (Courtesy of John S. Nichols; January, 1971).

Friendly Faces

Two of my good friends in Plainview, Danny McDowell and Dickie ("Duke") Crowder, spent most of my first day home with me. Seeing their friendly faces did me good, especially after hearing about the death of Steve Seigler.

Steve Seigler

Although Steve Seigler and I did not know each well, I liked him. And my meeting with him before going into the Army helped develop a bond between us that I did not fully understand. Somehow, in spite of his death, that bond continues today.

Steve's father, Dr. Gale Seigler, had given me physicals for athletics during my days at Coronado Junior High School and Plainview High

School. Now that I, too, am a father, I cannot imagine the terrible grief he suffered over Steve's death. Before Steve died, Dr. Seigler's wife and Steve's mother, Betty, had already died on April 25, 1969.

The funeral for Steve took place on February 22, 1971, at the Garland Street Church of Christ in Plainview. I did not follow through with my plans to attend; a decision I still regret to this day.

Figure 61 Steve Seigler in Vietnam watching a butterfly between missions (Courtesy of John S. Nichols; 1971).

Many years later I established contact with John S. Nichols, who served in Vietnam with Steve at Bear Cat (aka Long Thanh) with F Troop, 1st Squadron, 9th Air Calvary. I owe a debt of gratitude to John for telling me about his service with Steve and for sending me photos from Steve's tour of duty in Vietnam.

John and Steve flew together in an OH-6a LOH (light observation helicopter). They were together on February 13, 1971, when Steve died in Bien Hoa, South Vietnam, from a firearm accident after a mission. John and I both share the strong conviction that the accidental nature of Steve's death does not diminish his service or his sacrifice. My heartfelt desire is to honor Steve's memory as well as the memory of the many other Americans who served in Vietnam.

While I plan to return to Steve's story again later in this book, here I'd like to share with you some comments from John Nichols about Steve in Vietnam. In a letter John sent me via email, he wrote the following tribute to Steve:

> Each year, I think of him and the many other fine Americans that perished in that war. They all make me proud that I had the honor to serve with such heroes. I will always be grateful for his bravery and sacrifice as well as his kindness and humor. I would have flown anywhere with Steve. I trusted him with my life and he trusted me with his. Steve shared that fundamental quality that true warrior aviators had in common. You could look him in the eyes and knew without a doubt that if your bird was shot down, he was one of those brave men that would come and get you out "no matter what."[1]

Military Leave-Before-War Mentality

News of Steve Seigler's death intensified my pre-Vietnam leave time. Only those who have experienced going home on leave from the military

---

[1] Letter from John S. Nichols to Travis Monday. July 22, 2003.

before going to war can fully understand it. So many mixed feelings and thoughts assailed me that I felt compelled to stay busy doing and going in order to keep them from consuming me.

Day Tripper

One form of doing and going consisted of trips, mostly day trips. After traveling to Canyon, Texas, with Danny McDowell, I made trips to other Texas towns and cities, including Amarillo, Lubbock, Abilene, and Silverton.

Figure 62 The author, Travis Monday (left), in Plainview, Texas, with his friend, Danny McDowell (Author's collection).

Danny McDowell took me to West Texas University, where he was attending, and we also spent time in Amarillo. During one of our visits to Canyon, we toured the West Texas Museum, a place I had visited as a child. I had no idea at that time that I would eventually get heavily involved with the work of the Pioneer City-County Museum in Sweetwater, Texas.

These trips enabled me to talk with both relatives and friends, and to me that mattered.

Figure 63 The author with family members in Plainview during leave. Left to right: Teressa Monday, Travis Monday, Glynn and Wilma Phillips (Author's collection).

Movie Goer

My doing and going included watching movies. Having grown up as a movie buff, I continued that pattern during leave. On February 29th, some friends and I watched *The Private Life of Sherlock Holmes*. That night in my journal I wrote: "It was an excellent movie with superb acting and plot."

Catch-22, an antiwar movie based on Joseph Heller's book of the same name, stands out in my memory as a stimulus to my own growing antiwar thoughts and feelings. I watched this controversial movie with Charles

Montgomery and Kenneth Bond, and we had a good discussion about it afterwards.

Figure 64 The author (center) with his cousin, Trent Brown (left) and his friend, Charles Montgomery (Author's collection).

My patriotism and passion for freedom increasingly collided with a growing realization of the insanity of war. In Vietnam I would face the military war raging around me while also facing an inner conflict over the whole concept of war. *Catch-22* contributed to that inner conflict.

Charles Montgomery and I made several trips together and he later corresponded with me by mail while I served in Vietnam. He went with me to Abilene to visit my older brother, Derrell, who had surrendered to God's call to preach the Bible. Like Charlie, Derrell corresponded with me while I served in Vietnam, but during my tour of duty I didn't want to hear any preaching.

Last Full Day in Plainview

In my journal I summed up my last full day in Plainview, March 11th, as follows: "Charlie, Eldon, Larry Norman, Sherry, Kenneth, and I messed around for a while. Later Charlie, Sherry, and I went to the show. Made preparations for leaving tomorrow. Anticipate a lot of hard good-byes."

The next day I said good-bye to friends and family and traveled to Lubbock for the night.

California Dreaming

Early on the morning of March 13th, I left Lubbock for California, where I planned to finish my leave time with more family members. Later that day my dad, W. B. (Dub) Monday, Jr., met me at the airport. He received me warmly and offered me many words of encouragement during my visit.

In California I visited numerous other relatives. I particularly enjoyed seeing my cousin, Johnny Overstreet, and my granddad, W. B. Monday, Sr.

On March 16th, Dad and I, along with some of his friends, watched two movies: *Butch Cassidy and the Sundance Kid* and *M.A.S.H.* In many ways *M.A.S.H.* gave me a preview of Vietnam. Even though it was set in the Korean War rather than Vietnam, the craziness matched much of my Vietnam experience.

Oakland Army Base

The next morning, March 17th, I flew to Oakland. After my arrival at Oakland Army Base, the Army issued me my first jungle fatigues.

Much to my displeasure, I spent the next day pulling K. P. from 8:00 a.m. to 5:00 p.m. Afterwards I saw the movie, *Joe*, and then went bowling.

I spent the next five days pulling work details while waiting for a flight to Vietnam.

Leaving on a Jet Plane

Finally, on March 23rd, 1971, I left Oakland Army Base on a jet airliner. During my meeting with Steve Seigler shortly before I entered the Army, he told me that one of his favorite songs was "Leaving on a Jet Plane." John Denver wrote the song but the folk-singing group Peter, Paul, and Mary made it popular. Ironically, the last song I heard before boarding an airliner out of Oakland was – you guessed it – "Leaving on a Jet Plane."

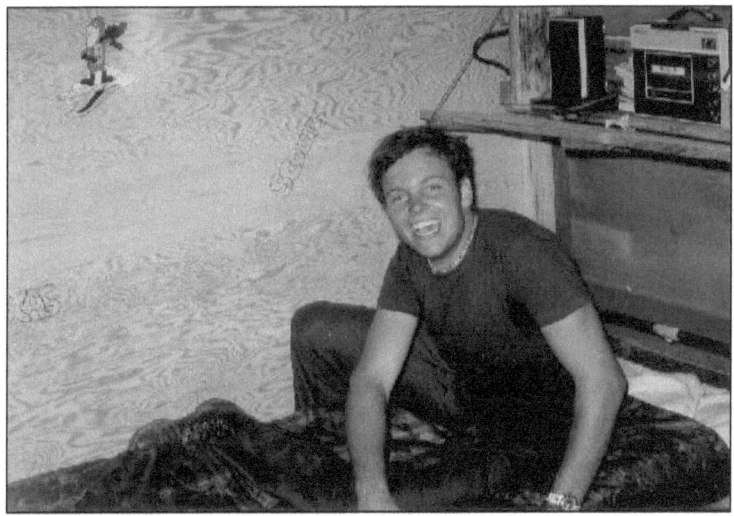

Figure 65 Steve Seigler in his "hooch" in Vietnam. Seigler liked the song "Leaving on a Jet Plane" written by John Denver and performed by Peter, Paul, and Mary (Courtesy of John S. Nichols; 1971).

My brief journal entry said, "Finally left Oakland. Flew to Anchorage, Alaska, and then headed across the Pacific for Japan."

Figure 66 Steve Seigler in Vietnam with his Air Cavalry Stetson (Courtesy of John S. Nichols; 1971).

Delta Developers -- Part 1

Figure 67 Lester Briggs at Tan Hoa with the 69th Engineer Battalion in Vietnam. The Vietnamese lady was one of several "hooch maids" who did laundry and cleaning for the soldiers for a monthly fee (Photo by author; 1971).

Although the flight to Japan and then Vietnam took only about twenty-four hours, I left the States on March 23rd and arrived in Bien Hoa, South Vietnam, at approximately 1130 hours on March 25th. Because of changes in the time zones, we had lost March 24th. Kind of sounds like "The Twilight Zone," doesn't it?

From Bien Hoa to Long Binh

During my tour of duty in Vietnam, I partied in various ways on many occasions, and I started partying on my first night "in country." At the end of my first day in Vietnam I recorded in my journal a few details about the trip to Bien Hoa, and then added, "Rode a bus to Long Binh. Went swimming, listened to a band, and then got drunk."

90th Replacement Battalion

According to Shelby L. Stanton, author of *Vietnam Order of Battle*:

> The 90th Replacement Battalion received, controlled, oriented, billeted, messed and processed in-country replacements for onward movement as well as personnel scheduled to return to the United States. It was located under the U. S. Army, Vietnam (USARV) at Long Binh for the duration of its service.[1]

Having lost my breath from the heat that greeted me when I stepped off the airliner in Bien Hoa, the sight of a swimming pool at Long Binh suited me just fine.

But something I heard on my first day at Long Binh didn't suit me at all. Reports of a mortar attack a few days earlier disturbed me. Wouldn't it be terrible to get killed before you even reached your unit?

I don't know about the accuracy of this report, but I also heard that several "newbys" (new arrivals in Vietnam) had skinned up their knees and elbows while trying to run to cover during a mortar or rocket attack and would, therefore, receive Purple Hearts. By the time I left Vietnam I would feel that I deserved a Purple Heart for all of my mosquito bites – just kidding!

---

[1] Shelby L. Stanton, *Vietnam Order of Battle* (New York: Galahad Books, 1986), 197.

Airborne Soldier with "Leg" Engineers

Fortunately, nothing happened to me at Long Binh that required a Purple Heart.

While I cannot remember all of the details of how I ended up in a "leg" unit instead of an Airborne unit, I do remember the essentials. By the way, *leg* refers to anyone in the Army who didn't earn the silver wings of a paratrooper. Those of us who earned our wings used the term in reference to non-Airborne personnel.

Before I arrived in Vietnam, probably while still in Jump School, I learned that my chances of making a parachute jump in Vietnam were extremely low. So when I learned that an engineer unit from Fort Hood, Texas, needed someone with my MOS (military occupational specialty), I said to myself, "Travis, since you're not likely to make any jumps even if you go to an Airborne unit, and since there is a unit from Texas nearby, why not make yourself available to that unit?" I indicated on some sort of form that I did not mind if the Army sent me to a non-Airborne unit. Whether or not that form had anything to do with the Army's decision to assign me to the unit from Fort Hood, I do not know, but that's what the Army did when it assigned me to the 69th Engineer Battalion.

Before my departure from Long Binh, the Army honored me with a couple of glorious opportunities to serve my country. On March 26th, I traveled to Camp Alpha in Saigon, where I cleaned latrines. The next day I worked a laundry detail. After a day of doing laundry, I had no objections to leaving Long Binh shortly before midnight for a place called Binh Thuy. I would later learn that my uncle, Joe Monday, had worked out of Binh Thuy Naval Base.

20th Engineer Brigade (Building Combat Power)

The 20th Engineer Brigade deployed to Vietnam in August, 1967, from Fort Bragg, North Carolina. It provided non-divisional engineer support for Military Regions III and IV, which included the Mekong Delta.

Later, after I reached my new battalion, I noticed members of my new unit wearing two different shoulder patches, including the red and white castle patch of the 20th Engineer Brigade. When I wore a patch, I chose the latter, but in a subdued black and green version designed for camouflage.

I've done a good bit of research on the matter, just to make sure I got it right, and the 20th Engineer Brigade patch is the correct patch for the 34th Engineer Group and the 69th Engineer Battalion for the time I served in Vietnam.

Figure 68 The shoulder patch of the 20th Engineer Brigade (Photo by author).

But the 20th Engineer Brigade patch was not the only one worn by members of the 69th Engineer Battalion. For those of you interested in these kinds of details, I'm including an excerpt from a letter sent to me by

Gerald T. Luchino of the Department of the Army, Institute of Heraldry, on November 29, 1990:

> Prior to August 1967, members of the Battalion wore the shoulder sleeve insignia approved for the U. S. Army Engineer Command, Vietnam. After that date, the Battalion was assigned to the 20th Engineer Brigade and that would have been the appropriate shoulder sleeve for wear in 1971.[2]

The Army later deactivated the 20th Engineer Brigade on September 20, 1971, but reactivated it at Fort Bragg, North Carolina, as an airborne brigade, on June 21, 1974. With a history that dates back to the American Civil War, the brigade continues today, living up to its motto: "Building Combat Power."

34th Engineer Group (Delta Developers)

Figure 69 Travis Monday in Can Tho, South Vietnam (Author's collection; 1971).

---

[2] Gerald T. Luchino, Letter to Author, November 29, 1990.

I chose the motto of the 34th Engineer Group, "Delta Developers," for the title of this chapter because it fits both my location and the work of our unit during my time in the Mekong Delta.

The 34th Engineer Group arrived in Vietnam from Fort Lewis, Washington, on March 27, 1967, and came under the command of the 20th Engineer Brigade in August of that same year. Initially located at Vung Tau, the group moved to Binh Thuy in February, 1969, and that's where I found it after my trip from Long Binh.

69th Engineer Battalion (Builders for Peace)

After my arrival in the Binh Thuy/Can Tho area, the 34th Engineer Group assigned me to the 69th Engineer Battalion at Can Tho. I would not remain in Can Tho for long.

The 69th Engineer Battalion left Fort Hood, Texas, for Vietnam in 1967. Arriving in-country on May 2, 1967, the unit soon went to work building roads and bases in the IV Corps area. As with other Army units, the 69th had a motto, and I still like it: "Builders for Peace."

In October, 1967, the battalion moved with the 34th Engineer Group from Vung Tau to the area of Can Tho and Binh Thuy.

During the Tet Offensive of 1968, Viet Cong forces assaulted the Can Tho Army Airfield, and the men of Headquarters Company of the 69th Engineer Battalion ended up in the thick of battle. The engineers stood their ground during the attack on January 31st, but five of them died defending the base. These American heroes were: CPL Ghalib Ahmed Abdullah, PFC Peter Michael Coleman, SP4 Richard Dale Hovland, SP4 James Richard McClintock, and SP4 Edward McNally. The Secretary of the Army later recognized the heroism of the men of Headquarters Company by awarding the company the Valorous Unit Award.

D Company, 69th Engineer Battalion

I briefly passed through Headquarters Company on my way to D Company. In my journal for March 29th, I wrote: "Moved to D Company area. Tomorrow I will do some more processing, and then head out for the camp where most of D Company is."

In a letter home that same day I said, "It's awful hot here and I've already got a sunburn."

Tan Hoa

Remembering the heat reminds me of the terrible thirst I felt during those first few weeks in Vietnam. No matter how much I drank, as soon as I finished, the thirst returned. I felt like I was sweating body fluids faster than I could take them in.

Thirst and all, I arrived at D Company's camp somewhere south of Can Tho and Binh Thuy on March 31st. We called this little work camp Tan Hoa, which somebody told me meant "Tent City." Indeed, most of us lived in six-man tents.

Tan Hoa stood next to a highway in a clearing with rice paddies and jungles nearby. Across the highway sat an ARVN (Army of the Republic of South Vietnam) Ranger camp and firebase. A little further south of us sat the village of Ky Tek (spelling uncertain).

Barbed wire surrounded Tan Hoa. More rows of barbed wire lay beyond the first row, with claymore mines laid out throughout the area. Just inside the first row of barbed wire, surrounding us, stretched a sandbagged bunker line with reinforced fighting positions spaced out along the line.

Tan Hoa was about the size of a square city block. Guard towers stood at each corner. In the motor pool the tower consisted of metal boxes called conexes stacked on top of each other, with sandbags around the edges of the top for the guard to sit behind, and with a wooden ladder leaning against the backside.

As I surveyed our defenses, I felt little comfort. "Travis," I said to myself, "there are actually people around here who want to kill you!"

Figure 70 Tan Hoa, south of Binh Thuy and Can Tho, in the Mekong Delta of South Vietnam. The author spent his first 4 months in Vietnam here (Photo by author, 1971).

Fire Support Base Mary Ann

Something else added to my concerns about people wanting to kill me. After my arrival in Vietnam, I learned that a few days earlier, on March 22nd, North Vietnamese Army (NVA) soldiers had overrun an outpost called Fire Support Base Mary Ann, southwest of Tam Ky in Quang Tin Province. The NVA soldiers had thrown satchel charges in the command bunker, and had knifed many of the American soldiers as they slept in their sleeping bags.

Remember that song from Basic Training about the Viet Cong? Part of it said, "He'll really do you in, if you let him catch you sleepin'."

Michael Amy

One of the first guys I remember meeting in D Company was a grader operator named Michael Amy. As a newby, I had no status whatsoever, but Amy didn't rub it in – at least not as bad as some of the others.

OJT with an M-16

Soon after my arrival at Tan Hoa, I began on-the-job training as a heavy equipment mechanic.

I cannot remember the rest of his name, but the guy who got me started as an engineer mechanic in Vietnam went by "Mac." On my second day of OJT Mac took me to a barge area where we replaced a hose on a front-end loader. I carried a toolbox in one hand and my M-16 in the other.

I'm not sure if Mac wanted to scare me since I was new in-country, or if he only wanted me to stay alert, but his warnings about snipers shooting at mechanics did nothing to ease my fears. He even said, "Sometimes one of us has to work while the other watches for snipers."

Guard Duty Among the Dead

Now I'm not trying to over dramatize this story, but after that day with Mac out at the barge, I pulled guard duty for the first time that evening. You'll never guess what sat behind the guard tower in the motor pool -- a graveyard!

While still in school in Plainview, I wrote a poem called, "Among the Dead." Here's how it goes:

> Slowly I walk through the graveyard alone,
> among the dead, far from home.
> No one can know my heart's dread as,
> drawn by some power,

I linger among the dead.

I know a fear no man has known,
yet I continue, continue to roam.
I notice the markers on many of the graves,
and I know that below
lie many of death's slaves.

Fog drifts among markers and leafless trees
as a vapor of horror to high degrees.
The cold winds moan as a sound of death.
Yes – the winds are cold
like death's own breath.

Why I am here I do not know,
but the spirits are laughing
as they scare me so.
Finally they bid me to go away,
knowing I'll return –
return to stay.

That poem proved somewhat prophetic, for there I sat pulling guard duty "among the dead, far from home."

Figure 71 Guard tower in the motor pool at Tan Hoa with graveyard behind it (Photo by author; 1971).

Attitudes Toward the War

In that far corner of the world called Vietnam, I soon discovered that many of the soldiers in my unit did not believe in the war. As I talked with them and increasingly realized that many of my fellow Americans back the World (United States of America) did not support either the war or us, my own attitude toward the war became increasingly negative, as did my attitude toward the military itself.

My attitude eventually became more positive, but any sane person knows that war itself, whether justified or unjustified, nurtures man's inhumanity to man, and promotes a certain amount of insanity.

In behalf of the men I served with in Vietnam, I want the reader to understand that most of them did their jobs even though many of them did not believe in the war.

I've talked with lots of other Vietnam veterans from the earlier years of that war whose experiences differed significantly from mine. But by the time I got to Vietnam, the tide definitely had turned against the war. In some other units things may have been different, but I know what kinds of attitudes I encountered. The men I knew in Vietnam, regardless of their attitudes toward the war, served their country and deserve the gratitude of their fellow Americans.

Annoying Artillery

Shortly after my arrival at Tan Hoa, I discovered that combat zones can get rather noisy. The artillerymen at the firebase near our camp must have worn out their 105s firing them so much. At the very least they seemed determined to wear out my ears, especially when they fired over our heads.

At first I couldn't understand how the men of D Company could act so calm with artillery frequently firing nearby, and I wondered how any of us would get any sleep. My newfound friends told me I'd get use to it, and I did. Before long the firing of those 105s didn't even faze me.

And when I realized that the artillery helped keep the Viet Cong away from our camp, I learned to love it.

On April 7th, I stood guard at the edge of the jungle for a general's helicopter. I do not remember his name.

Early Impressions of Vietnam

On April 9th, I wrote a letter to Mother, which I quote in part:

> You ought to see the streets of these cities. There are literally hundreds of motorcycles within view all the time. Driving is a mess. The average environment of these people is about equal to our ghettos and slums.
> American influence is everywhere . . . . I guess we have done them some good in the areas of medicine and education. The unit I'm in now is building a highway.
> This is a beautiful place. If it were not for the war, it would be a tropical paradise.

Part of what made the Mekong Delta a tropical paradise of a sort was the availability of fresh coconuts and bananas. The watermelons were smaller than those in Texas but quite tasty, and the bananas were still green even when ripe. And although I never learned to like coconut milk, I loved the fresh white meat inside the shell.

Watching the War

The jungles and rice paddies of the Mekong Delta were ripe with the reality of war. During my first few months in Vietnam, I *saw* a lot of combat – from a distance. For example, on May 11th, American helicopters and airplanes went after some targets near us. In my journal for that day I said that they were "firing like hell all around us."

On that same day I also wrote: "I think a door gunner was hit as a 'copter landed with someone who was wounded. We are still on alert with our weapons at ready. The VC may try to hit us before the rains get much worse."

About a week later, on May 18th, I wrote the following: "Watched Cobra gun ships and airplanes and jets use napalm, rockets, bombs, and machine gun fire on a nearby area all morning long. We strongly expect to be hit tonight or tomorrow night."

During my first four months with D Company, I had other similar experiences of watching American aircraft in action. And on other occasions we went on alert with warnings of possible enemy attacks.

On the occasion mentioned above on May 18th, we expected to get hit hard by a large enemy force. Since we had a small camp primarily designed for building highways and maintaining equipment, our defenses could not have withstood a large enemy assault.

Figure 72 Travis Monday in front of his tent at Tan Hoa in South Vietnam. The wooden building in the background was the mess hall (Author's collection; 1971).

I remember thinking about my namesake, Colonel William Barrett Travis, commander of the Alamo. Like Travis and the other Alamo defenders, I made up my mind to put up a good fight even if we got overrun by enemy forces. That night, when the attack seemed imminent, I gathered all of the ammunition and hand grenades that I could find, grabbed my flak jacket and helmet, and stationed myself in a sandbagged fighting position. Based on what I had been told, I fully expected to die that night.

After waiting all night for the enemy attack, the next morning I got word that Cobra gun ships had driven away the enemy force. Since that time I've wondered if the threat was real or if, perhaps, somebody played a cruel joke on me. Whatever the case, I took the threat seriously and felt great relief when the danger passed.

During those times of frequent alerts and multiple air strikes, I often watched OV-10 Broncos in action. I suspect that they were part of the Black Ponies out of Binh Thuy.

I also watched Cobras in action, and they impressed me as awesome aircraft with incredible firepower. I'm confident that the various flight crews of the different aircraft I watched in Vietnam helped us survive, and I'll always be grateful for their support.

Malaria Medevac

Another type of support consisted of medevac helicopters. Their flight crews saved many lives during the Vietnam War.

For example, we had a soldier in our unit who caught malaria. I have photos of men in our unit carrying him to the helicopter pad and of a medevac helicopter taking off with him on board.

Figure 73 A soldier at Tan Hoa with malaria being carried by stretcher to a helipad for evacuation (Photo by author; 1971).

Those same photos show the setting for another medevac situation involving a Vietnamese civilian.

Figure 74 Another photo of the evacuation of the soldier with malaria. At this same location the author witnessed the evacuation of a young Vietnamese girl whom the Viet Cong had blown up with hand grenades (Photo by author; 1971).

Mekong Princess

One day exploding hand grenades broke the boredom of working in the motor pool, and we immediately went on full alert. The explosions came from the nearby village of Ky Tek, where six Viet Cong soldiers had tossed hand grenades into the hooch of a Vietnamese family.

ARVN Rangers made contact with the enemy assassination squad and the sound of their M-16s briefly filled the air. Someone told me that the Rangers had killed three of the Viet Cong but that three more had escaped.

By that time I had taken my position at the top of the guard tower in the motor pool, where I made sure the M-60 machine gun was ready to fire.

I don't remember who climbed the ladder with me, but we checked our clackers in case we needed to set off our claymore mines. We also had our M-16s locked and loaded.

We had received orders to guard the helicopter pad near our guard tower. A medevac helicopter would soon land to pick up a little girl who had survived the attack on her family.

Moments later a group of soldiers carried the young child by my position on either a stretcher or a poncho – I don't remember for sure. As they carried her past the left front side of the guard tower, I looked directly at her mangled form. I had never seen what hand grenades could do to a person.

Seeing that little girl made me angry, but then a sort of emotional numbness kicked in as I turned my attention back to protecting the helicopter pad. I did not expect the girl to survive.

By this time an olive drab green UH-B1 medevac helicopter had arrived. The men who carried the injured girl loaded her into the aircraft.

Sometime during this process, I spotted three armed men in black pajama-like clothes running across a distant clearing toward the edge of the jungle. I knew they were the remnants of the Viet Cong assassination squad. During Jump School I had written in my journal that I hoped I would not have to kill anyone, but after seeing that little girl I wanted to kill her attackers. Indeed, I wanted to blow them away with the M-60 machine gun, but they disappeared into the jungle before I could fire a shot.

A short time later I learned that the little girl died soon after the helicopter lifted off.

Years later memories of that incident moved me to write a poem. I called it, "Mekong Princess," and it goes like this:

> I saw a little girl dying –
> hand-grenade fever and shrapnel-itis.
>
> With an O.D. green stretcher underneath,
> they loaded her lacerated life onto a chopper –
> quick help for one quietly dying.
>
> She died in the air o'er the Mekong Delta.
>
> I saw her killers running –
> and tried to fire a shot,
> but since they reached the jungle's edge
> frustration is all I got.
>
> Little princess, you were not pretty to see.
> Why does your mangled image continue with me?
>
> I saw a little girl dying
> from what grenades can do.

> Her family – they won't miss her –
> you see –
> they all died too.

War Raging Within

The tragic death of that little Vietnamese girl greatly increased my internal conflict. As mentioned earlier, in Jump School I had written in my journal, "I just hope I don't have to kill anybody." Now, in spite of my growing antiwar sentiments and my talk of making love instead of war, I wanted to kill some Viet Cong. I wanted revenge for what they did to that little girl and her family.

We hear a lot of talk these days about terrorists. The Viet Cong were some of the worst terrorists in human history. In their book, *Inside the VC and the NVA*, Michael Lee Lanning and Dan Cragg assert:

> Although isolated incidents of terrorism by Allied troops received much more attention in the world media, the fact remains that murder, torture, and intimidation were routine tactics of the VC/NVA. This was formally outlined in their COSVN Resolution Number 9, published in July 1969.[3]

As this comment suggests, the NVA and the VC were the bad guys, not us.

In recent years I've read about accusations of atrocities committed by the 69th Engineer Battalion. Although I sometimes resisted the authority of those who outranked me and even spoke against the war, I never

---

[3] Michael Lee Lanning and Dan Cragg, *Inside the VC and the NVA* (New York: Ballentine Books, 1992), 187.

suspected anyone in the 69th Engineer Battalion of participating in atrocities.

Getting By With a Little Help from My Friends

The internal struggles that plagued me sometimes seemed unbearable, but I got by with a little help from my friends, including my best friend in the 69th Engineers, Bob Dils, and another good friend, Lester Briggs.

I also remember Albert Long, Terry McBride, and many others, and I am proud to have served with them.

A Friend from Plainview in Vietnam

Another friend of mine in Vietnam, Bobby Phillips, came over with the U. S. Navy as a helicopter mechanic. Stationed at Binh Thuy Naval Base, not far from the places where I served with the 69th Engineer Battalion, he stopped by to see me numerous times. On other occasions I visited him in Binh Thuy.

Bobby and I graduated from Plainview High School together, and we loved trading insults during high school. After he joined me in Vietnam, we enjoyed renewing our insult-trading activities. In particular I liked calling Bobby a worm and telling him that the worm is the lowest form of life on the planet. I'm not going tell you what he called me because that way I get the last word.

Since Bobby was in the Navy and I was in the Army, we had plenty of new material to work with in our efforts to insult each other.

Figure 75 Terry McBride of Indiana (wearing hat and with hands in pockets) in the motor pool of D Company, 69th Engineer Battalion (Photo by author; 1971).

Figure 76 Travis Monday in the motor pool at Tan Hoa (Author's collection; 1971).

Figure 77 Robert (Bob) Dils, the author's best friend during his time with D Company of the 69th Engineer Battalion (Photo by author, 1971).

Figure 78 A soaking wet Travis Monday at Tan Hoa after a ride in an uncovered jeep during a monsoon rain (Author's collection; May 3, 1971).

Figure 79 Another view of Tan Hoa in the Mekong Delta of South Vietnam (Photo by author; 1971).

Figure 80 Left to Right: Travis Monday, Lester Briggs, Albert Long, and Bob Dils at Tan Hoa (Author's collection; 1971).

Delta Developers -- Part 2

As previously mentioned, in Vietnam I experienced plenty of fear. Just knowing that people want to kill you works on you even if you experience little or no combat. I didn't know it at the time, but fear had invaded my soul, and I would later carry it inside of me when I returned to the United States.

Fear and anger often go hand-in-hand, and I felt angry much of the time. Sometimes I took my anger out on those who outranked me whether they deserved it or not, and I often wanted nothing more than to get out from under their authority.

But the fear and anger didn't bother me nearly as much as the boredom.

Battling Boredom

Those who have never lived in a war zone sometimes think of war as almost constant excitement, but most war veterans will tell you that they spent a lot of time battling boredom.

Sometimes on guard duty I'd get so bored that I actually wanted something to happen. And the drudgery of working in the motor pool day after day did not match the ideas of glory and excitement I had seen in war movies.

One tiring reality of military life was the ever-present dominance of olive drab green. Green clothes, green hats, green tents, green trucks, green jeeps, etc., along with the boredom of the daily routine in the motor pool, inspired me to write a poem called, "O.D. Blues."

> I'm working for my Uncle Sam;
> the place I'm at is called Vietnam.
> The pay I get – it's not much,
> and the privacy –
> well, there ain't no such.
>
> The clothes I wear are all O.D. green;
> sure gets old when that's all you've seen.
> Mosquitoes here are as bad as can be;
> without my repellant they'd finish me.
>
> Twelve hours a day ain't much fun,
> sweating and cursing in the hot, hot sun.
> To see a flush toilet would sure be fine,
> but if I did it would blow my mind.
>
> Always trying to hide so I won't have work.
> Gotta put in for a transfer – where's the clerk?
> Every day I get a little more lazy.
> To stay in this Army, I'd have to be crazy!

I must have already been crazy because I made a decision that could have cost me my life.

Door Gunner

I don't remember who came up with the idea to volunteer for Door Gunner School. At Fort Leonard Wood I succeeded in talking several guys into going to Jump School with me, but I don't remember if I did the same thing with Door Gunner School. The primary instigator might have been me or someone else, but four of us decided to volunteer. You need to understand that helicopter door gunners in Vietnam had a tendency to get killed. There you would sit, with little protection, while enemy soldiers made you a target. My friend Eldon Box from Plainview survived his tour of duty as a door gunner, so maybe I would too.

With hindsight I now find myself grateful that our CO (commanding officer) turned down our request. On May 20th I wrote in my journal, "Four of us put in for Door Gunner's School today, but Captain Palmer disapproved them all so we won't get it."

Figure 81 Travis Monday (left) and Bob Dils jokingly point to a sign that encouraged soldiers to sign up for more time in the Army (Author's collection; 1971).

I didn't give up without giving it a second try. On May 23rd I wrote, "Talked to the Sergeant Major about being a door gunner. I may be able to get it without re-upping. I'll take it if I can."

Re-upping meant re-enlisting for more time in the Army. I've got a photo of Bob Dils and me standing in front of a 34th Engineer Group sign that says, "Re-Up!" I wanted into Door Gunner School, but not that much!

Joe Monday and the Seawolves

While I'm on the topic of door gunners, my uncle, Joe Monday, the one who served on the USS Forrestal, also served as a door gunner with the Navy Seawolves.

Figure 82 Joe Monday served with the Navy Seawolves in Vietnam (Author's collection).

The Seawolves of HA(L)-3 primarily provided aerial support for the Navy SEALs and for the PBRs (patrol boats riverine). In his book, *Seawolves: First Choice*, Daniel E. Kelly explains:

> We worked with a lot of different units in combat besides our own. The 9th Infantry, Koreans, Australians, the Vietnamese Army (ARVNS), Marine Corps Recon, and the Green Berets. Our reputation with them was high, and we wanted to keep it there.

However, most important to us were the river patrol boats (PBRs) and the SEALs.[1]

I knew nothing about the Seawolves until Joe and I got together in Vietnam. A Navy man at Binh Thuy told me that he knew Joe. A short time later, Joe paid me a visit. He said very little about the Seawolves then, but shortly before his death in August of 1998, he let me interview him about his Navy exploits.

Figure 83 Joe Monday (left) with his brother, W. B. (Dub) Monday, Jr., on the occasion of their mother Gladys Perry's funeral (Photo by author; Nov. 18, 1997).

The occasion for the interview was the funeral of Joe's mother and my grandmother, Gladys Perry. For years I'd been trying to talk Joe into letting me record an interview with him, but he kept putting me off. After

---

[1] Daniel E. Kelly, *Seawolves: First Choice* (New York: Ivy Books, 1998), 66.

Grandmother's funeral, I approached Joe about an interview, and once again he tried to get out of it. I then said, "Joe, now don't you go and die on me without giving me that interview."

A strange look came over Joe's face, and then, with the urging of his wife, Janelle, he finally consented. Since he died of cancer a short time later, I suspect that he knew that he might not be around much longer.

Figure 84 A Navy version of the UH-1B helicopter (Photo by author).

When I asked Joe if he served as a door gunner in Vietnam, he replied, "Yea, I used a door-mounted mini-gun." He went on to explain that he flew in UH-1B Hueys, sometimes referred to as "Slicks."

Joe also spoke of flying in an HH1K, a Navy version of the Huey, bragging, "It can pick-up an Army Huey. It was much more powerful."

At one point in the interview, Joe told me the following story:

> We took a hit. We had inserted the SEALs and we came around behind them because the VC were coming around back. We were

laying down cover and killing a few VC when the pilot and co-pilot got hit. I got in there and landed the helicopter. I used to fly test flights in those things back at Binh Thuy, so I was familiar with what was going on.

While doing research for this book, I found a picture of Joe on the internet as a part of Det 7 (Detachment 7), and in the photo his eyes are closed but he has a smile that looks so much like the Joe I remember.

Kelly said something in his book that reminded me of Joe's powerful laugh. "Seawolves was a good-humored outfit. When we weren't fighting, we were laughing. We had to in order to cope with the lifestyle."[2]

Humorous Incident

In regard to laughing, something happened in our company area one day that still makes me smile. During mail call, a soldier started shouting hysterically and waving his arms around with something in one of his hands.

At first I couldn't understand his words, but when I moved closer I heard him shouting, "Oh my God! I've been drafted! They've sent me a draft notice! What if they send me to Vietnam?"

D Company Dogs

I don't' know if they got drafted or not, but we had dogs in the 69th Engineer Battalion in Vietnam. Soon after the Army assigned me to D Company, I learned that a dog named J. B. had been with our outfit for over a year or longer. Apparently J. B. got his name from a CO named Captain J. B. Summers. Our J. B. may have been our unit's second J. B.

---

[2] Kelly, 245.

We had another dog named J. J, which stood for "Janis Joplin." I'm not sure how long J. J. had been in-country, but someone said she was on her second tour of duty. I watched J. J. give birth to a litter of pups under the bunk next to mine in our six-man tent out at Tan Hoa. We gave J. B. credit for fathering the litter.

I picked a brown female puppy from J. J.'s litter and named her Mickey. We bonded instantly. Mickey didn't last long. After about a month she ate rat poison and died.

Figure 85 Travis Monday's little puppy, Mickey, in South Vietnam (Photo by author; 1971).

Incident at Binh Thuy North

D Company moved three times during the seven months I spent with them. While at our third location – a place we called Binh Thuy North, I had an experience that still haunts me today.

Soon after dark one night, I began walking toward a guard tower to take my turn at guard duty. I soon discovered that someone had moved the ladder, so I had no way to reach my position.

Since I knew not to leave my post and since the field phone was beyond my reach at the top of the tower, I decided to guard the area from the ground. I chose to stand in a dark, shadowed area so no one could see me.

Shortly after I took my position in the shadows, I saw three Vietnamese clad in black clothing crawling through the barbed wire near my position. About the time I spotted them, they stood up and walked swiftly past the guard tower – obviously aware that no one was in the tower. They must have seen me walk away when I discovered that the ladder was missing.

With only a few yards between them and me, I knew I had to act quickly. As mentioned earlier, I had heard about the sapper attack on Fire Support Base Mary Ann, during which American soldiers were knifed in their sleeping bags while others were blown up in bunkers with satchel charges.

My most obvious choice was to shoot the three men before they could do any damage, but my situation wasn't that simple. With the war winding down, restrictions on firing our weapons had become increasingly strict. Even though I had caught the men coming through the wire into our base, I had been told that I could not shoot anyone unless I first saw that they had weapons. The darkness made that impossible. And I also knew that, even if they appeared unarmed, they might be carrying weapons and explosives under their clothing.

Of course, if I failed to stop these men, they might carry out some sort of attack and kill me or some of my friends.

As these thoughts raced through my mind, I made a decision. While still hidden by the darkness of both night and shadows, I put my M-16 on full automatic and fired a burst of ammo over their heads. In case they returned fire, I immediately hit the ground and rolled over to a new position ready to fire a second burst if needed.

The three men instantly turned around and ran back past the guard tower and back through the barbed wire with incredible speed.

A few minutes later, the Sergeant of the Guard drove up in a jeep demanding to know if I had fired my weapon. After I told him yes, he demanded to know why.

"Because I don't like men in black running around me in the dark," I replied. Then I explained about the missing ladder and why I couldn't use the field phone in the guard tower.

What really hacked me off was what happened next – absolutely nothing! Three men had come through our defenses and into our camp, yet no one questioned me further about the incident. It was as if it had never happened. That made absolutely no sense to me.

Years later I talked with a Navy SEAL about the incident, and he told me that I made the right choice for those circumstances. That helped me feel better about it.

Even now I do not know if I stopped an attack or if I just scared off a few thieves, but I do know that I caught three intruders sneaking into our camp and prevented them from carrying out their plans.

The 69th Engineer Battalion Goes Home

When we first heard that the 69th Engineer Battalion would soon return to Texas, we rejoiced at the prospect of getting out of Vietnam. But the date of departure kept getting changed, so we kept getting disappointed.

Because of the delays in the standing down of the battalion, I felt sure I'd return to Fort Hood, Texas, with it. My leaders told me that anyone who had been in-country for six months or more would go home with the 69th. Although I met and exceeded the six-month criterion, the Army decided to send me up north to another unit instead of letting me return to the World.

In a letter home I explained:

> Well, the 69th Engr Bn is leaving 'Nam by the 15th of November, and by that time I will have left all of my friends behind to go to a new unit alone to make new friends and spend my remaining five months in a different part of Vietnam.
>
> I'm going to the 101st Airborne Division. You know – the Screaming Eagles.

One More Promotion

Late in October, before I transferred to the 101st Airborne Division, the Army promoted me from PFC to Specialist 4th Class.

Figure 86 Bobby Phillips (holding puppy) and Travis Monday in Vietnam at Binh Thuy North (Author's collection; 1971).

Figure 87 Travis Monday (left) with Bob Dils at Binh Thuy North (Author's collection; 1971).

Screaming Eagles in Vietnam

Figure 88 The shoulder patch of the 101st Airborne Division Screaming Eagles (Photo by author).

> Specialist Monday, welcome to the
> 101st Airborne Division (Airmobile).
> We are happy to have you
> join the Screaming Eagles.
> --Letter from 101st Abn Div
> Headquarters

Before I received the letter welcoming me to the 101st Airborne Division, I made the journey from Binh Thuy to Saigon by truck, then from Saigon to Da Nang by C-130, and from Da Nang to Hue and Phu Bai in a truck convoy.

Even though I had heard about the terrible fighting in Hue during the Tet Offensive of 1968, the amount of battle damage still evident in 1971 amazed me. That must have been one heck of fight.

101st Airborne Division (Airmobile)

Any military historian worth his salt knows about the Screaming Eagles' famous stand against the Germans at Bastogne during World War II. When the Germans had them surrounded, they demanded that the outnumbered American paratroopers surrender or face annihilation. General McCullough replied with one word: "Nuts!"

Even with my growing desire to get out of the Army and out of Vietnam, I still felt a certain amount of pride over becoming part of the famous Screaming Eagles.

The 101st Airborne Division arrived in Vietnam prepared to carry out traditional airborne operations, but the nature of the Vietnam War resulted in a major transition for the Screaming Eagles. By the time I joined them in late 1971, they had added the word "Airmobile" in parentheses to their name.

This change meant that the 101st Airborne Division (Airmobile) had shifted its primary method of delivery to the battlefield from parachutes to helicopters. My discovery that hardly anyone else in my unit wore jump wings surprised me. Imagine my reaction when I heard other men in my battalion say repeatedly, "Airborne! Airmobile! Airbubble!"

On November 9th I wrote in one of my letters home: "Well, I've already moved and am now in the 101st Airborne Division (Screaming Eagles), and believe me it's quite a change. I'm in the mountains now and not far from the ocean."

326th Engineer Battalion

Figure 89 Distinctive Unit Insignia of the 326th Engineer Battalion. The lettering means "The Task is Ours."

Within the structure of the 101st Airborne Division, the Army assigned me to HHC, 326th Engineer Battalion (Airmobile).

The 326th Engineers began on July 23, 1918, as part of the 101st Division, and then was demobilized later that same year. On June 24, 1921, the Army reconstituted the unit as the 326th Engineers (Combat) as an element of the 101st Division. In August of 1942, shortly after America began its first paratrooper training program, the unit became the 326th Airborne Engineer Battalion.

Members of the 326th participated in the airborne assault into Normandy and later into Holland. They stood with other Screaming Eagles at Bastogne. After receiving two Presidential Unit Citations, the 326th was deactivated on November 30, 1945.

On May 15, 1954, the Army reactivated the 326th Engineer Battalion at Fort Jackson, South Carolina. A short time later, the battalion moved to Fort Campbell, Kentucky, to support the 101st Airborne Division.

Company A deployed to Vietnam on August 3, 1967, with the rest of the battalion arriving on November 24, 1967.

Camp Wilkinson

Upon arriving at HHC, 326th Engineer Battalion, I learned that Camp Wilkinson had been built by Navy Seabees.

Figure 90 Two of the author's great uncles, Dean (left) and Lee Monday. Dean Monday served with the Navy Seabees in World War II, landing on Iwo Jima ahead of the Marines (Author's collection).

I've already mentioned my uncle Joe Monday, who made a career out of the U. S. Navy. I also had a great uncle named Dean Monday, who served in the Navy with the Seabees during World War II. He landed at Iwo Jima ahead of the Marines. After he left the Navy at the end of World War II, he spent most of the rest of his life in Pampa, Texas, with his wife, Nelda.

Camp Wilkinson, located two km southeast of Camp Eagle, was named after CMI Jack W. Wilkinson of the U. S. Navy. Wilkinson died from "friendly fire" when a stray Army 105 mm artillery round exploded in his vicinity.[1]

One major difference in Camp Wilkinson from the setting I knew in the Mekong Delta was that we had a large mess hall. While I liked the facility, I didn't like it when I had to pull K. P. again, something I had not done down south.

Figure 91 The mess hall at Camp Wilkinson near Phu Bai, where the author served with Headquarters Company, 326th Engineer Battalion, 101st Airborne Division. The motor pool is in the background (Photo by author; 1971).

While at Camp Wilkinson, I could no longer wear my boonie hats, which I greatly preferred over the baseball-style caps of the 326th Engineer Battalion.

---

[1] Michael P. Kelley, *Where We Were in Vietnam* (Central Point, Oregon: Hellgate Press, 2002), 5-549.

Rats

One thing Camp Wilkinson had in common with all of the locations where I lived in the Mekong Delta was an ample supply of rats. Rats pestered many Americans in South Vietnam. Military historian Ronald H. Spector says, "Rats were a constant nuisance in most forward areas in Vietnam."[2] Without questioning Spector's conclusion, I'd say rats were also a constant nuisance in many of the rear areas.

While I saw plenty of rats in the Mekong Delta, the ones in and around Camp Wilkinson seemed bolder and meaner. Down south our dogs helped us control them, but not up north where I saw no dogs.

Because of the rats at Camp Wilkinson, I did not sleep much during my last few months in Vietnam. They pestered me almost every night after I got in my bunk.

The walls inside our hooch had a layer of plywood coming up about halfway to the ceiling, and our bunks were lined up with one side against the walls. At night the rats would climb up between the outer wall and the plywood, peer over the edge of the plywood until they saw I had fallen asleep, and then jump on my bunk.

Like some of the other soldiers, I feared getting rabies from a rat if bitten.

Looking back, it almost seems comical, but I slept with a hammer in one hand and a knife in the other, and with a flashlight nearby. If I heard rats crawling up the wall, I'd bang on the plywood to knock them back

---

[2] Ronald H. Spector, *After Tet: The Bloodiest Year in Vietnam* (New York: The Free Press, 1993), 47.

down. If they jumped on my bunk, I'd try to get them with my knife. I fought to stay awake because I knew they'd jump on my bunk if I went to sleep. That wasn't a very good way to spend the last few months of my all-expense paid vacation to Vietnam.

One night while pulling guard duty in a rat-infested bunker, I noticed through the corner of my eye that a rat had crawled into the sleeping bag of another soldier. I walked up to him and gently said, "Now, I don't want you to panic, but I think I just saw a rat crawl into your sleeping bag."

Figure 92 A bunker in which the author pulled guard duty during December, 1971. Rats often visited these bunkers and in some cases the rats lived in them (Photo by author).

No sooner had those words left my mouth than my fellow soldier screamed loud enough to wake up people back in Texas. He also ripped open his sleeping bag totally destroying the zipper. Instead of taking turns guarding our assigned area, we both stayed awake for the rest of the night.

While I'm on the topic of guard duty, I noticed another big difference between the Phu Bai area and the Mekong Delta. I told Mother in a letter dated November 17th, "I had guard duty last night and almost froze. I didn't think it got cold in 'Nam, but it does in this part."

A New Set of Friends

Living and working together in a war zone makes a certain amount of bonding inevitable, and before long I had a new set of friends in the 326th Engineer Battalion. Sergeant Shannon Gillis, my immediate supervisor, treated me well and we became good friends. He came from Georgia. I also remember William McCormick, Ronald McFarland, Patrick Parlow, a soldier named Sanchez, and a Zuni Indian from New Mexico whom we called Yazzi.

My best friend up north was John G. Owens from North Carolina. John had volunteered for Vietnam so that he could get out of Germany. He made a good start on teaching me to play the guitar. Since my days in the 1st grade in Hereford, Texas, when my brother Derrell took guitar lessons, I had wanted to learn how to play. Hearing Eldon Box play his guitar while I was home on leave had rekindled that desire.

In a letter home dated November 26, 1971, I wrote:

> I've got a guy teaching me to play the guitar and I'm loving it. I bought an old guitar with no strings for $5.00 and put strings on it. It's not a very good one, but it's something to learn on. Owens, the guy teaching me, has a twelve-string guitar. He just got here from Germany about the same time I got here from down south.

Generator Mechanic

Although my regular Army job consisted of working as a heavy equipment mechanic, I spent some time up north working with Owens on generators. I volunteered to work on generators so that I could work with Owens, but it meant being on call 24 hours a day. Sometimes we worked on generators in the motor pool and at other times we worked on them out on the bunker line.

Working on the bunker line involved some risk since we were sitting ducks for snipers, but no one ever shot at us. Sometimes when Owens got called out to the bunker line at night, I'd go with him so that he would not have to go alone.

Those generators kept John and me awful busy most of the time, but we did not have to pull guard duty or K. P. Later, after I was no longer assigned to the generators, I had to resume pulling guard duty and K. P. Sure didn't make me happy.

Tape from Friends Back in the World

Some of my friends in Plainview sent me an audio cassette tape during my time at Camp Wilkinson. On the tape Danny McDowell offered me lots of words of encouragement. Dickie Crowder and some other friends did more of the same.

My favorite part of the tape consisted of the singing of Jo Wilson. I particularly liked hearing her sing the popular James Taylor song, "You've Got a Friend."

Going Home Early, But . . .

My tour of duty in Vietnam would have lasted until March of 1972, but President Richard Nixon's decision to get most of our troops out of the country as soon as possible meant I'd probably have my tour cut short.

At first I heard we might leave Vietnam about a month early. Then I heard we might go home on December 26th, a prospect that thrilled my homesick soul.

I shouldn't have gotten my hopes up. As I reported to Mother in a letter dated December 11th: "The rumors about the 26th were true for most people, but not for me. Almost everyone will leave this unit this month. I've been selected to stay until 14 Jan 72 for equipment escort."

Trip in an LST

I'm not sure of the date, but I rode in an LST along the coast of Vietnam as part of an equipment escort. Although my memories lack clarity, I believe we traveled down the coast to Da Nang to deliver the equipment. I liked riding in the LST and had no problems with seasickness.

Afterwards, we returned to Camp Wilkinson.

No Hope for Me – Bob Hope That Is

By December 20th, 1971, our work had slowed considerably. No longer working as a generator mechanic, I started having K. P and guard duty again.

Then we received word that Bob Hope would perform at Camp Eagle. I wrote home saying, "We're going to have the Bob Hope Christmas Special here pretty soon. I'll be there."

I only thought I'd be there because when Bob Hope presented his Christmas Special to the 101st Airborne Division on Christmas Eve, 1971, I missed it because of guard duty. I've often said that I guarded Bob Hope – from a distance.

Since I couldn't see the show in person, I asked a friend to film the show for me on my Yashica Super 8 movie camera. The footage doesn't have sound, but you can see Bob Hope, Jim Neighbors, Miss America, and others.

Christmas Eve and Christmas, 1971

In some ways I'm glad I missed the Bob Hope Christmas Special because of something that happened on guard duty that Christmas Eve.

I don't know who started it or why, but someone pulling guard on the bunker line started popping flares into the air. Then, someone else fired some rounds into the sky, including some tracer rounds. Before long, glowing tracers and bright flares lit up the sky in a way that reminded me of a huge fireworks display.

I had never seen anything like it before, and I've not seen anything like it since. The event inspired me to write the following poem, called "Phu Bai Fever":

> It started with a couple of flares,
> and then a few rifle shots,
> and then atmospheric saturation.
>
> Hawkins eyed me in fear.
> Were the NVA attacking?
>
> Then we understood.
>
> We locked and loaded our M-16s
> and blasted away at the sky.
> The enemy must have thought us crazy.
> Camp Eagle encircled by crazed Americans
> firing weapons and popping flares.
>
> Walt Disney watched with envy as
> we laughed and screamed and
> joined the celebration of madness.

The exhilaration of those moments didn't last long, and when the light of a new day dawned that Christmas morning, Hawkins and I waited anxiously for the truck that would take us back to Camp Wilkinson. That truck never arrived, so I spent part of Christmas morning, 1971, humping my M-16 and an M-60 machine gun several miles back to camp.

Adopting Orphans

Contrary to stereotypes of American soldiers in Vietnam as baby-killers who spent much of their time committing atrocities, in truth our men and women in Vietnam, as in other wars, sought to do good in many different ways.

During my time with the 326th Engineer Battalion, a Catholic priest arranged for us to have an Adopt-an-Orphan Day. The men in my unit willingly accepted his invitation to spend a day with a child from a nearby orphanage. I think all of us, regardless of our attitudes toward the war, felt good about that experience.

When we left Vietnam, the Catholic priest remained in-country with those orphans, and I've often wondered what happened to him and to those kids. I believe NVA forces overran that whole area soon after we left.

Award Recommendation

I still have in my possession a form signed by our CO Captain Robert L. Herndon recommending me and some other soldiers for a Bronze Star. Included with the recommendation was the following statement:

> These individuals while attached to my unit rendered outstanding contributions toward the overall mission of this unit and thus of the Division. Their conduct, performance, and manner of service were exceptional, in keeping with the highest traditions of the military service, and are most deserving of the meritorious service award for which they are recommended.

I never received the award and I did not deserve it, but I appreciate the recommendation.

Good-Bye Vietnam

On January 14, 1972, I traveled from Phu Bai to Da Nang. Before leaving the Phu Bai area, I remember giving away a brand new 12-string guitar for the simple reason that I had too much stuff to carry. While standing in a long line loaded down with gear, I saw a Vietnamese citizen standing nearby. I asked him if he wanted my guitar. He nodded, and I handed it to him. He enthusiastically thanked me, but I was so tired of carrying it that I felt I should thank him.

After we arrived in Da Nang, I did a lot of out processing, which meant standing in long lines and signing lots of papers.

Finally, on January 16th, I boarded my Freedom Bird for the United States of America.

Figure 93 The entrance to Camp Wilkinson, where the author served with the 326th Engineer Battalion, 101st Airborne Division (Photo by author; 1971).

Figure 94 Travis Monday in the back of a 5-ton Army dump truck in Vietnam (Author's collection; 1971).

Figure 95 Travis Monday (front center) arrives back in the United States after his tour of duty in Vietnam (U. S. Army photo; January, 1972).

Figure 96 Photo of Travis Monday taken while he was enroute to Plainview, Texas, for 30 days of leave after his tour of duty in South Vietnam (Author's collection; January, 1972).

An Eagle with Sky Soldiers

I barely remember my leave time in Plainview after Vietnam, but I know I spent a lot of time partying.

After leave I reported to Fort Campbell, Kentucky, where I would continue serving in HHC, 326th Engineer Battalion, 101st Airborne Division (Airmobile).

While at Fort Campbell, I'd get to jump with some of the Sky Soldiers of the former 173^d Airborne Brigade, but first I'd have to make some major adjustments in my life.

Fort Campbell, Kentucky

Before I explain those adjustments, let's take a quick look at some of the history of Fort Campbell, Kentucky, and the surrounding area. Fort Campbell was named after Brigadier General William Bowen Campbell, a former governor of Tennessee who participated in the storming of Monterey in the war with Mexico in 1846. Construction on the post, located between Clarksville, Tennessee, and Hopkinsville, Kentucky, began on February 4, 1942. At that time they called the new installation Camp Campbell.

The Army renamed the post Fort Campbell during April, 1950.

On September 21, 1956, a ceremony at Fort Campbell marked the reactivation of the 101st Airborne Division, which had been deactivated after World War II.

During the 1960s the 101st Airborne Division left its home at Fort Campbell to join the fight in Vietnam. I had entered the division and the 326th Engineer Battalion late in 1971 in time for the return to Fort Campbell in early 1972.

Fort Donelson

While at Fort Campbell, my love of history motivated me to visit the old Civil War installation near Clarksville, Tennessee, known as Fort Donelson. I did not know at that time that two of my Monday relatives had fought there with the Confederacy.

Figure 97 General Ulysses S. Grant during the Civil War. He led the Union troops to victory at Fort Donelson in Tennessee, where the author's relatives, Shelby Y. Monday and Malchi Monday served the Confederacy with E Company, 26th Tennessee Infantry.

The Battle of Fort Donelson took place on February 14-16, 1862. My relatives, Shelby Y. Monday and his brother Malchi, served with E

Company, 26th Tennessee Infantry. They had enlisted in the Confederate Army on July 13, 1861, at Camp Cummings near Knoxville, Tennessee.

Civil War buffs will remember that Ulysses S. Grant got the name, "No-Surrender Grant" at the Battle of Fort Donelson, where, after a hard fought battle, he led the Union Army in a victory over the Confederates.

As to the fate of my relatives, Malchi Monday became a prisoner of war after the battle. Shelby, after sustaining a wound during the battle, died in a makeshift military hospital in Clarksville, on the site of the current Austin Peay State University. He survived for about a month before succumbing to pneumonia.

Figure 98 Confederate re-enactors at Fort Concho in San Angelo, Texas (Photo by author; December 7, 2002).

Malchi and Shelby had a younger brother named Henry who later fought for the Union in E Company of the 10th Cavalry. He participated in the Battle of Nashville in 1865.

My Monday relatives had migrated from North Carolina to Eastern Tennessee and had settled in the area of Rhea County and Cumberland County. Before the move to Tennessee, my ancestor Arthur Monday had served against the British during the American Revolution.

My Major Malfunction

I don't think my Monday ancestors would have approved of my misbehavior at Fort Campbell after my return from Vietnam. Those of us who reported to my unit after leave didn't do much at first. Instead, we showed up for roll call in the mornings, then we'd hit the local bars.

I'm not sure why the Army let us get away with that sort of behavior, but I think the idea was to allow us a little time to readjust to life in the States. In my view that approach hurt us more than it helped us, but I accept full responsibility for my actions.

After Vietnam I sort of went crazy, and the Army sort of let me – for a while. For the sake of my fellow paratroopers, allow me to say it like this: My life had become a major malfunction.

Finally the time came to crack down on our unruly behavior. The Army needed to make an example out of some of us, and I became one of the chosen few.

My behavior had worsened to the point that I would leave Fort Campbell and not return for days at a time. I repeatedly went AWOL (absent without leave) and thought nothing of it. I got away with this misbehavior long enough that when it got me in trouble it caught me by surprise. The Army fined me and restricted me to the company area. So I rebelled and went AWOL again. When I finally returned to Fort Campbell to "face the music," the Army took away most of my pay for several months, increased my restrictions, and busted me down to E-1 – the lowest rank in the Army.

Drug and alcohol abuse had impaired my judgment. And don't forget that I mixed a lot of bitterness and resentment toward authority in there with the alcohol and other drugs.

A New Jumpmaster

My brother, Derrell, a Baptist minister, had been trying to talk some sense into me for a long time, primarily through letters. In Vietnam I read his letters, tore them up, and said to myself, "I don't want anybody preaching to me!"

Figure 99 Travis Monday (left) with his grandmother, Gladys Perry, and his brother, Derrell Monday (Author's collection).

After I got fined and busted down to E-1, I received another letter from Derrell, but this time I paid attention. As with his earlier letters, he spoke of my need for Jesus Christ.

Sitting alone in the barracks one night, I prayed and admitted to God that I had messed up my life. I asked him to forgive me for all my wrongdoing and help me make a fresh start. God heard my prayer. Almost instantly I felt the warmth of God's love and somehow knew that he had forgiven me.

As a child I had often heard a well-known verse from the Bible, John 3:16, which says, "For God so loved the world, that he gave his only begotten Son, that whosoever believeth in him should not perish, but have everlasting life."

Although I had heard it before, in the barracks that night the story of Jesus Christ's death and resurrection took on a new meaning for me. I realized that his death on a cross made it possible for me to start over.

Later I wrote a poem about God's forgiveness called, "Just for the Record," and it reads as follows:

> If there were only records, Lord,
> of all I've said and done;
> if there were only records, Lord,
> I'd be a doomed man.
>
> But forgiveness was, forgiveness is,
> and forgiveness will always be,
> your paper shredder for records of sin –
> your Christ-kept file on me.

With forgiveness came an awareness of God's presence and a life-changing experience of his grace. My anger and bitterness melted away and in their place God gave me a feeling of tranquility and acceptance beyond anything I had experienced before.

Then I remembered a Gideon Bible I had picked up in Vietnam in a chapel in Can Tho. I had grabbed it primarily because it was free, and I liked free stuff. Now I felt a strong desire to read my Bible, and as I did, the words took on a new power and meaning almost beyond description. I could sense the truth of every word I read, and I knew that God's truth had set me free.

You see, I had found a new Jumpmaster, Jesus Christ, and I knew that I could jump into a whole new way of life, and that he would take care of me. I was ready to follow him into any battle and to follow his orders without question.

Figure 100 Travis Monday in his barracks at Fort Campbell, Kentucky, reading his Bible (Author's collection).

A Changed Life

The changes that took place in my life after that night astonished my friends as well as the officers and NCOs in charge of me. Instead of getting drunk or high, I started going to chapel services and attending Bible studies. After I told some of my fellow soldiers about what Jesus had done for me, some of them also found help by trusting in him. Of course, some of my friends thought I had totally lost it, but that didn't bother me.

I soon discovered a group of Christians known as the Navigators, and they started teaching me about the Christian life. One of them, Mike McCoy, helped me grow spiritually. Mike and his wife, Judy, welcomed me into their home, and Mike started teaching me how to study and memorize Bible verses, and how to walk with Jesus.

Figure 101 Travis Monday in his khaki uniform at Fort Campbell, Kentucky (Author's collection).

I made a lot of new friends in the Navigators, and I developed a strong liking for a guy a named John Sands. He seemed to live above the circumstances rather than under them, and the joy of knowing Jesus Christ personally seemed to overflow out of his life.

My job performance also improved. In a letter home dated October 27, 1972, I said, "I've been working hard and doing very good at my job. I've started going to church and am taking a Bible study course also."

In spite of getting in trouble because of my misbehavior, as a result of the adjustments in both my attitudes and actions, I received an award for Outstanding Soldier of the Month. By the time I got out of the Army, I had regained all of my rank through accelerated promotions.

Back in the Harness Again

Remember that song by the singing cowboy Gene Autry called, "Back in the Saddle Again"? Well, I soon found myself back in a parachute harness again.

After not jumping during my tour of duty in Vietnam, and after learning that the 101st Airborne Division had switched from parachutes to helicopters, I did not know if I would get another chance to jump.

But then I found out that the Division had not completed the transition to air mobility, so I would get to jump. Since my own company did not jump, I'd have to find someone else to jump with, and that's how I connected with the Sky Soldiers of the former 173^d Airborne Brigade.

173^d Airborne Brigade at Fort Campbell

The Army first formed the unit as the 173^d Infantry Brigade in 1917, in time for the unit to deploy for France. After World War I, the Army demobilized the brigade at Camp Dix, New Jersey, during January, 1919.

After going through a series of changes, the reactivated unit became the 87th Reconnaissance Troop of the 87th Division. Under this new designation, the unit experienced combat in World War II as part of General George Patton's Third Army.

On March 26, 1963, the Army activated the unit on Okinawa as the 173^d Airborne Brigade. Because of the many parachute jumps made after the unit formed, the Nationalist Chinese called the paratroopers of the 173^d "Sky Soldiers," and that name stuck.

In May of 1965, the 173^d became the first regular American Army unit sent to the Republic of South Vietnam. During the unit's tour of duty, it conducted the only major combat parachute jump by Americans in the Vietnam War.

Figure 102 The shoulder patch of the 173d Airborne Brigade (Photo by author).

The Sky Soldiers endured almost six years of continuous combat in Vietnam, earning four unit citations as well as many other awards. These awards did not come cheap. As Airborne historian E. M. Flanagan, Jr., says, "The 173d paid an enormous price, however, losing 84 officers, 2 warrant officers, and 1,526 soldiers to combat. Another 8,500 officers and men were wounded in action."[1]

---

[1] E. M. Flanagan, Jr., *Airborne: A Combat History of American Airborne Forces* (New York: Presidio Press Book published by Ballentine Publishing Group, 2002), 387.

After leaving Vietnam as a part of President Nixon's major troop withdrawals, the 173^d was deactivated on January 14, 1972, at Fort Campbell, Kentucky. After deactivation the 173^d Airborne Engineer Company became Company C, 326th Engineer Battalion, 101st Airborne Division (Airmobile). By virtue of that change, they officially became Screaming Eagles, but the men of the unit still took great pride in identifying with the 173^d Airborne Brigade and with the label, "Sky Soldiers." That's why I named this chapter, "An Eagle with Sky Soldiers."

Company C, 326th Engineer Battalion, 101st Airborne Division (Airmobile) set up camp in the barracks right next to mine. They had earned the silver wings of the Army paratrooper, and they soon returned to jump status.

When I learned that Company C was jumping, I asked to jump with them, and the Army granted my request.

Jump Number 6

The first couple of times I tried to jump with the men of C Company, the jumps got cancelled. I still remember that at least one of my fellow paratroopers suggested that I might be jinxing them, but no one pressed that possibility very far.

Somehow I've lost the exact date of my sixth jump, but in a letter home dated October 8, 1972, I said, "I'm supposed to jump Wednesday the 11th unless, of course, something happens again."

Without knowing the exact date, I do know that my first jump after Vietnam required that I jump with a toolbox, which I had not done in Jump School. The weight of that toolbox, combined with all of my other equipment, caused me to make a poor exit from the C-130. That's the only jump during which I remember brushing against the fuselage of an aircraft after making my exit. By the grace of God, I did not hit the fuselage hard and suffered no injuries, but it gave me a slight scare.

The rest of that jump went well, including my first effort at lowering my toolbox on a line before landing.

101st Airborne Division's Welcome Home Ceremony

Figure 103 General William C. Westmoreland made a jump in Korea in the same year that the author was born -- 1952 (U. S. Army photo).

The 101st Airborne Division (Airmobile) had been the last U. S. Army division to leave Vietnam. On April 6, 1972, the Army held a welcome home ceremony for us. That's more than most Vietnam veterans got back then, but it lacked meaning for me since it did not come primarily from the civilian population.

I remember standing under a hot sun to hear a couple of speeches. Although I don't remember who went first, Vice President Spiro T. Agnew and General William C. Westmoreland spoke to us.

Westmoreland, who died during the writing of this book, had made a jump in Korea in 1952, the year of my birth.

Sergeant Denny

While at Fort Campbell I worked under a motor sergeant by the name of Sergeant Billie E. Denny. A former Green Beret, he had chased Che Quevera in South America. Under his supervision, I spent a lot of time inspecting motor vehicles. I liked Denny, and appreciated his efforts to help me improve as an Army engineer mechanic.

Dirty Trick

I guess you could call it a dirty trick. We had this one guy in our company who kept coming in late at night drunk as a skunk. As this pattern continued, we all got fed up with his behavior and decided we needed to do something about it.

Someone suggested that we play a trick on him. So one night, after he again arrived under the influence, we waited for him to pass out on his bunk, and then we did our dirty deed. Bunk and all, we carried him outside the barracks to a grassy area where we sometimes held formations. And that's where we left him.

When our hung-over friend woke up the next morning, he couldn't figure out how he ended up outside in his bunk bed. The rest of us got a good laugh out of it, and our friend decided to change his habits.

Jump Number 7

My second jump with the men of C Company differed from my previous jumps because we made it at night – my first night jump. Because of the darkness, night jumps present certain challenges to paratroopers, most of which have to do with visibility and landing. More specifically, misjudging the distance to the ground before preparing to land can cause a jumper to crash and burn.

In preparation for my first night jump, our leaders and several of my more experienced friends told me how to judge the distance to the ground by observing the horizon. By watching the tops of the trees, I could tell when I had about 100 feet left between me and mother earth. I could also expect to see men on the ground with flashlights trying to help us judge the distance.

Remembering the advice of my fellow paratroopers, I jumped into the night sky from a C-130 on March 27, 1973. Afterwards in a letter home I wrote, "I made my first night jump Tuesday. It was kind of scary, but really fun. It was the best jump I've ever had. No one was hurt except for getting a little muddy."

Like my first jump at Fort Campbell, my second jump there was an Equipment Jump.

A New Set of Orders

Men and women in all branches of military service know the experience of receiving a new set of orders and then acting on them. Since I had trusted in Jesus Christ as my Lord and Savior, I had a new set of orders – the Bible.

With the help of Mike McCoy and the Navigators, I began studying and memorizing the Bible and adjusting my life accordingly. The more I studied the more I realized how bad I had blown it. In one of my letters home I wrote the following confession:

> I'm finding my greatest joy in the Lord and am striving more and more every day to become a better Christian. God only knows how far off course I've strayed, but at the same time he has taught

me much that will be helpful. I pray every day that God will take my life and make it useful. I've been such a poor example.

Remembering past failures could have driven me into deep despair, but God's forgiveness replaced my feelings of hopelessness with hope. As I studied the Bible, my hope increased and I developed a desire to share it with others. Mike McCoy and some of the other Navigators started teaching me how to tell others about Jesus Christ.

I soon realized that my new set of orders included talking to other soldiers about the Lord, and I found many opportunities to act on those orders. In one of my many letters to Mother I told her of one such opportunity: "This coming Sunday I will be giving my personal testimony before the congregation of Central Chapel here on post. I hope you will pray for God to help me speak in such a way as to draw others to Christ."

Studying the Bible also increased my awareness of my own need for Christ. After my night jump with the men of C Company I wrote, "Without Christ I can only crash and burn."

Figure 104 Travis Monday standing in front of a front-end loader at Fort Campbell, Kentucky (Author's collection).

Figure 105 The author's bunk bed and locker in the barracks at Fort Campbell, Kentucky (Author's collection).

Figure 106 Travis Monday drove around in this contact truck fixing broken down vehicles at Fort Campbell, Kentucky (Photo by author).

Figure 107 The author (right) with a fellow soldier in the woods of Fort Campbell, Kentucky (Author's collection).

From Airborne to Chairborne

> Suffer hardship with me, as
> a good soldier of Jesus Christ.
> --Paul the Apostle (2 Tim. 2:3, NASB).

God's work in my life turned me into a good soldier in the U. S. Army, but beyond that I wanted to become a good soldier of Jesus Christ. As I thought and prayed about my new life as a soldier of the Lord, I began to sense that God wanted me to spend the rest of my time on earth doing three things: preaching, teaching, and writing. In order to follow my new set of orders, I needed a better education. For me that meant going from Airborne to Chairborne, that is, going to college.

Lure of the Lone Star State

Before my discharge from the Army, I seriously considered going to college at Austin Peay State University in Clarksville, Tennessee, and even began making the necessary preparations. Because of my desire to write, I planned to major in English.

Then I changed my mind. I decided to return to the Lone Star State for college. I narrowed my choices to either Wayland Baptist University in Plainview, or Hardin-Simmons University in Abilene. After much prayer, I chose Hardin-Simmons, where my brother Derrell attended. With Derrell's help, I gained acceptance into the program at Hardin-Simmons in time for the fall semester of 1973.

Plainview Pit Stops

After leaving the Army on August 21, 1973, I traveled home to Plainview. There I enjoyed seeing family and friends again, but some of them seemed shocked that I planned to study for the ministry. I had given them plenty of reasons to react that way.

Before going into the Army, I had attended Bethel Baptist Church in Plainview. After I got out of the Army, and under the leadership of Pastor Gene Joplin, the church agreed to license me to the Gospel Ministry.

Figure 108 Bethel Baptist Church in Plainview, Texas, licensed the author as a minister of the Gospel of Jesus Christ (Photo by author).

Later that fall I returned to Plainview to speak at Bethel Baptist Church. When I spoke there I openly confessed my abuse of alcohol and other drugs. I also told the congregation how Jesus Christ had changed my life for the better.

Throughout my college years, I made frequent pit stops in Plainview, mostly to visit my family. During the visits I developed the habit of visiting Steve Seigler's grave in Plainview City Cemetery. I also visited the graves of Jimmy and Roger Awalt.

Figure 109 The grave of Steve Seigler in the Plainview City Cemetery in Plainview, Texas (Photo by author).

ROTC Rejected

When the leaders of the ROTC program at Hardin-Simmons learned that I was a Vietnam veteran, they tried to sign me up for ROTC. Without the slightest hesitation, I turned them down.

Even though I left the Army on good terms, I had no intention of ever entering the military again. And after three years in the Army, including a tour of duty in Vietnam, college life seemed like a picnic.

Abilene, Texas and Hardin-Simmons University

I liked living in Abilene, Texas, and I loved Hardin-Simmons University. Abilene's friendly atmosphere made living there a great pleasure, while HSU seemed like heaven on earth.

Sure, even college life at Hardin-Simmons could get rough at times, like when I struggled my way through the Greek Class of Dr. Ray Ellis, or when I took Dr. Zane Mason's history tests, but I loved the Christian environment and the academic setting. I still get a good feeling every time I visit the campus of Hardin-Simmons University.

Monday and Mitton

Figure 110 Travis Monday (left) with his best friend at Hardin-Simmons University, John Mitton (Author's collection).

God blessed me with many good friends at Hardin-Simmons, including people like Robert McKinnon, Allen Estes, Mark Cook, Gene Takaki,

Chuck Gafford, Jim Way, Ted Spear, Robert Bergin, Becky Bridges, Bob Ellis, Bobby Munoz, Pat and Ann Heard, and many others.

But my best friend at Hardin-Simmons, without question, was John Mitton. John and I roomed together in Anderson Hall, and we shared many adventures, as well as some significant ups and downs.

At one point John and I became a two-man ministry team by leading church fellowships in churches near Abilene. We often did humorous skits, and at times we made up our own material spontaneously during our live performances. Sure wish someone would have recorded them. Well, maybe its better that they didn't.

Better than the Best

Figure 111 The author with his future wife, Pamela Jean Krebs (Author's collection).

Pamela Jean Krebs became a better friend than my best friend, John Mitton; she became my wife. I met her at a college fellowship at First

Baptist Church in Abilene, and it thrilled my soul to learn that she, too, was a student at HSU. She had transferred to HSU from Pacific Lutheran College in Tacoma, Washington.

After dating for a couple of years, Pam and I spent the summer of 1976 at Mercer Island, Washington, where I served as an apprentice pastor to Rev. Roy Belcher, pastor of Mercer Island Baptist Church.

On August 14th of America's Bicentennial Year, Bro. Belcher tied the knot for us before we returned to Abilene to finish college. Other than Jesus Christ, Pam is the best person that ever happened to me.

Figure 112 Travis and Pam Monday married in Mercer Island, Washington, on August 14, 1976 (Author's collection).

The Fall of South Vietnam

The fall of the Republic of South Vietnam interrupted the good life at Hardin-Simmons. Even during those good days in Abilene, I thought about Vietnam every day, but most of the time I could keep it in the background of my life and focus on the present and the future.

News of the collapse of South Vietnam in 1975 brought my Vietnam experience back into my life in a way that demanded more attention. Although I had gone through a time of viewing America's involvement in Vietnam as a mistake, something inside of me cried out against our failure to come to the aid of our ally.

On May 4, 1975, I wrote President Gerald Ford a letter expressing my feelings. I did not actually believe that he would read it, but I figured somebody would. In the letter I expressed concern that our nation had slipped into a sort of isolationism that would prevent us from fulfilling our God-ordained obligation to make this world a better place.

PTSD Previews

Most people have heard of PTSD (Post Traumatic Stress Disorder). PTSD can hit anyone who has suffered significant trauma, not just war veterans. But most of my exposure to it has come primarily from interacting with other war veterans and from personal experience.

At Fort Campbell, Kentucky, I showed numerous signs of PTSD, but after putting my faith in Jesus Christ, the effects seemed minimal. I did not recognize some of my own symptoms but I knew that I carried the war around inside of me every day.

I later expressed this awareness in a poem called, "Returning."

> I have returned
> to monsoons of madness;
> to "dung lai," Da Nang,

and "number ten thou;"
to mosquitoes and mortars;
and, of course,
to my tent.

I once thought I'd leave here
and never return, but
this place is timeless,
and so is my tour.

After my move to Abilene to start college, I occasionally got a bit jumpy when I heard a car backfire, and the sound of a helicopter usually caused flashbacks, but these symptoms didn't last long and they didn't keep me from doing well in school or from holding down a job. Although the fall of South Vietnam in 1975 caused my own PTSD to worsen, I usually just prayed about it and moved on.

Abilene Writers Guild

During my days at Hardin-Simmons I discovered and joined the Abilene Writers Guild. Attending conferences and spending time with other writers strengthened my desire to write.

The president of the guild, Juanita Zachry, gave me some much-needed encouragement and helped convince me to enter one of their contests. I decided to enter three poems in the non-professional category, two of which dealt with Vietnam. John Igo, the Texas State Poet at that time, judged the poetry. When I learned that I had won first place, second place, and honorable mention with my three poems, it definitely made my day.

The first place poem, called "Vietnam Romance," says:

Grace the land
with blood and guts;
spatter life's liquid

to water the plants
that cover the naked earth.

Smoke smell stenches loudly nostril that
die so slowly that
death seems hidden in death.
The pale forecast of tomorrow
anchors itself in now's sore moment
and kills the taste of
beans.

Sometimes the dream
of home still lingers
amidst these fumes of hell,
and dulls the senses
to this air of death
for a moment.

After reading my winning poems during an awards ceremony, one of the ladies in the guild said to me, "You certainly are a dirge of war." I didn't know if she meant that as a compliment or an insult.

Dr. Lawrence Clayton

Dr. Lawrence Clayton, an English professor at Hardin-Simmons, did more to encourage me as a writer than any one else in my life. He helped me in class as a professor, and he helped me out of class as a friend and mentor.

Through Dr. Clayton's influence, I edited the college magazine, *The Corral*. I served as the literary editor, and Becky Bridges worked with me as the art editor. Becky's father, Dr. Julian Bridges, taught sociology at Hardin-Simmons.

Even after I left Hardin-Simmons, I corresponded with Dr. Clayton, and he always urged me to keep writing.

Shortly before Dr. Clayton's death, I saw him at the Spade/Renderbrook Ranch south of Colorado City, Texas. I had just preached an outdoor wedding for a couple of our church members from Calvary Baptist Church of Colorado City, and I heard a voice saying, "Why I believe that's one of them Monday boys."[1] I then spotted Dr. Clayton walking toward me wearing a black cowboy hat and a grin as big as Texas.

Return to Kentucky

Marshall Walker, the Director of Religious Activities at Hardin-Simmons, also made a difference in my life. Through his influence, I got involved with the Baptist Student Union and began going on mission trips to Mexico and to other states in the U.S.A.

Since I had developed a liking for Kentucky while stationed at Fort Campbell, Kentucky, I gladly returned there as a part of a college ministry team.

During that trip our team worked at Carlton Winton's church in Frankfort, Kentucky. Winton took us to Churchhill Downs, the capitol building, Daniel Boone's grave, and the Colonel's House. At the Colonel's House, an elaborate and beautiful version of a Kentucky Fried Chicken restaurant, we saw Colonel Sanders.

Not counting the spiritual blessings of that trip, the highlight came when we received certificates signed by Governor Julian M. Carroll declaring us honorary Kentucky Colonels. Since I was named after

---

[1] Dr. Clayton had also taught my brother, Derrell Monday, at Hardin-Simmons University in Abilene, Texas.

Colonel William Barrett Travis, commander of the Alamo, I thought to myself, "Now people can call me 'Colonel Travis'."

Church Work

Along with going on mission trips during college, I also served on the staff of some churches. I've already mentioned working as an apprentice pastor to Rev. Roy Belcher at Mercer Island Baptist Church. With my limited musical abilities, it still amazes me that I worked as Minister of Music and Youth at Prairie View Baptist Church in Anson, Texas, a small town north of Abilene.

One of the members of Prairie View Baptist Church who stands out in my memory is Sheriff A. C. Middleton, who attended our church faithfully.

In Abilene I served as Minister of Youth for Temple Baptist Church. Pam and I found it easy to love Rev. H. B. Terry, Jr., and his wife, Faye. After Bro. Terry learned that Pam didn't think humans should eat black eyed peas, he kidded her about it from the pulpit.

Bro. Terry's strengths included hospital and grief ministry, and the Lord taught me a lot about those ministries through him. I didn't know that I would eventually serve the Lord as a hospital chaplain in San Angelo, Texas. I now believe that the Lord used Bro. Terry to help prepare me for that ministry. Years later the Lord also used Chaplain Milton Tyler of San Angelo to help move me into fulltime hospital ministry.

Graduation from College

I graduated from Hardin-Simmons University with a Bachelor of Arts degree in Bible and English on May 8, 1977. Pam finished in December of that same year with a Bachelor of Science degree in Physical Recreation. Although she completed her studies in December, 1977, she had to wait until May, 1978, for her formal graduation.

Working as a Surgical Orderly

While waiting for Pam to graduate from HSU and while also working as Minister of Youth for Temple Baptist Church, I landed a job at Hendrick Medical Center in Abilene as a surgical orderly.

For the most part I enjoyed working in surgery, and watching operations didn't bother me. Not, at least, most of the time. When a young burn victim came in for skin grafts, I always got woozy and faint. That happened to me several times with that same burn victim.

I know that those kinds of responses sometimes bother people who've never been to war, but in my case I believe the Vietnam War was a factor. I'll explain why later.

From Abilene to Forth Worth

After college Pam and I moved to Fort Worth, Texas, where I planned to attend Southwestern Baptist Theological Seminary. Pam found a job working for Olmstead Kirk Paper Company and I went to work for Wackenhut Security Corporation as a security guard.

Soon after we got settled into our new home in Fort Worth, I discovered that an Airborne Infantry unit of the Texas Army National Guard was located in nearby Arlington, Texas. That discovery would make a significant difference in our lives.

Figure 113 Pam and Travis Monday on their wedding day (Author's collection).

Figure 114 Travis and Pam Monday during their college days at Hardin-Simmons University in Abilene, Texas (Author's collection).

Figure 115 Travis Monday on the campus of Hardin-Simmons after his graduation on May 8, 1977 (Author's collection).

Figure 116 Pam Monday with her mother, Ellie, at Hardin-Simmons after her graduation in May, 1978 (Author's collection).

Airborne Again!

Figure 117 Army paratroopers jump from a C-141 Starlifter (U. S. Army photo).

When I left the Army in 1973, I never thought I'd even consider enlisting for military service again, but learning of the presence of an Airborne unit in Arlington, Texas, helped change my mind.

This change didn't come without much prayer and thought. Pam and I talked it over. I began to wonder if God might want me to re-enter the military as an Army chaplain. Perhaps a two-year commitment to the Texas Army National Guard would enable me to discern God's will.

I finally made up my mind; I would go ALL THE WAY one more time. I would be *Airborne again!*

36th Airborne Brigade

Figure 118 Shoulder patch, jump wings, and distinctive unit insignia of the 143d Airborne Infantry Regiment, 36th Airborne Brigade (Photo by author).

By entering the Texas Army National Guard unit stationed in Arlington, Texas, I became a member of the 36th Airborne Brigade, a unit descended from the famous 36th Infantry Division of World War II.

This connection would reemerge later in my life through contact with a man named W. F. Matthews, who survived 3 ½ years as a prisoner of the Japanese in World War II. He too had joined the Texas Army National Guard and had served with the 36th Infantry Division. But his unit, the 2nd Battalion, 131st Field Artillery, unlike most of the 36th Infantry Division, did not fight in the European Theater. Instead, they fought in the Pacific against the Japanese on Java.

In my new unit, I wore the famed blue and gold Texas T Patch of the 36th Infantry Division, but with a blue and white Airborne tab over it. As a native-born Texan, I took great pride in wearing that patch on my left shoulder while also wearing as a combat patch on my right shoulder the eagle of the 101st Airborne Division.

143d Airborne Infantry Regiment

Along with the prospect of jumping again, the Texas Army National Guard unit in Arlington appealed to me for another reason. My growing pride over my service with the Army Engineers had not destroyed my unfulfilled desire to serve in the Army Infantry.

Maybe my longing to earn the Green Beret of the Special Forces would not be satisfied, and perhaps I'd never wear the Black Beret of the Army Airborne Rangers, but by becoming a part of the Army Airborne Infantry, I would know that I had trained and served with some of the best soldiers in the world.

On April 3, 1978, I wrote in my journal:

> Spent most of this day in Dallas talking about and preparing to enter the 1st Bn (Abn) 143d Inf. of the Texas National Guard. My physical exam will be tomorrow morning at 6:30. If I pass it I'll be enlisted tomorrow. Hope to jump again at the end of this month.

After passing a physical and working through all the paperwork, I became a member of Company B, 1st Battalion (Airborne), 143d Infantry, on April 4th. I had signed up for two more years as an Army paratrooper.

My new unit had a coat of arms and a motto. The motto embodied a goal that matched my convictions: "Arms Secure Peace." In my mind a strong military should always aim beyond military conflict to the goal of peace, but Jesus Christ is our best hope for actually achieving peace.

On April 27th, 1978, my journal entry read: "I'm excited about being *Airborne again*. As I continue to seek God's will concerning what specific area of ministry I should be in, the military chaplaincy is increasingly in my mind."

82nd Airborne Division

Today our nation has only one complete division of Army paratroopers – the 82nd Airborne Division. The All Americans of the 82nd Airborne Division first earned their place in history during World War II.

Figure 119 The shoulder patch of the 82nd Airborne Division – the All Americans (Photo by author).

In some form or fashion, our unit in Arlington was linked to the 82nd Airborne, so we wore the same burgundy (or red) beret as them. We also trained with them at Fort Chaffee, Arkansas, by serving as their opponents in war games.

During the Iranian Crisis, someone in our unit told me that if the 82nd went to Iran and started losing men in battle, we would replace their casualties.

Missing a Jump

When I joined the 143d Airborne Infantry, I expected to make a jump that same month, but an unexpected health problem interfered. Soon after moving to Fort Worth, I had found a job working for Wackhenhut Corporation as a security guard. One assignment consisted of walking around a gin all night watching for any signs of fire. Much to my surprise, both of my knees became painfully inflamed.

I hated to do it, but I called my National Guard unit and told them I'd have to miss the jump. I would not get another chance to jump until our upcoming summer camp at Fort Chaffee, Arkansas.

Fortunately, my inflamed knees cleared up and in June I made the trip to Fort Chaffee.

Jump #8

Figure 120 The paratroopers of the 143d Airborne Infantry unit often jumped from CH-47 Chinook helicopters (U. S. Army photo).

On June 20, 1978, I jumped for the first time in five years. As we waited on Arrowhead DZ for a CH-47 Chinook helicopter to take us up, one of my fellow paratroopers made fun of me for being a preacher. In a sarcastic tone of voice he said, "Hey, preacher, pray for me."

Like Flip Wilson, maybe the devil made me do it, for I replied, "I'll pray for you; I'll pray that your parachute doesn't open!"

The response of my antagonist surprised me. Instead of responding with some sort of smart alert comment, he turned as white as a ghost and said nothing.

By the time we loaded into the Chinook and jumped, darkness had descended, so my first jump with the 143d Airborne Infantry was also my second night jump. In my journal I wrote, "The jump went beautifully for me although a couple of guys hurt their shoulders. We jumped from 1500 feet."

M-60 Machine Gun Qualification

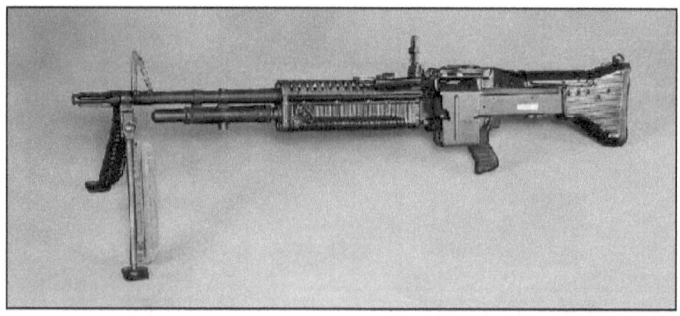

Figure 121 The author qualified on the M-60 machine gun at Fort Chaffee, Arkansas, while serving with the Texas Army National Guard (U. S. Military photo).

Although I learned how to load and fire M-60 machine guns during my years in the Regular Army, and even used them on guard duty in Vietnam, as an Army mechanic I had never officially qualified on them.

While at Fort Chaffee in the summer of 1978 serving as a member of an infantry unit, I fired for qualification. In my journal entry for Sunday, June 25, I wrote, "Day before yesterday I accomplished the first part of my M-60 machine gun qualification. It was too hot and one gunner fainted from heat exhaustion."

The following week I qualified expert on the M-60. Afterwards several of us got to fire up a bunch of old ammunition just for the fun of it. The only thing I didn't like about the M-60 was changing the barrel when it got too hot.

Jump #9

Figure 122 The author made his first jump from a C-141 Starlifter while serving with the Texas Army National Guard (U. S. Army photo).

On Saturday, June 24, 1978, before I qualified on the M-60, I made my ninth jump. I described the experience in my journal as follows:

> Yesterday I made my first jump out of a C-141 jet aircraft. The heat was terrible before and after boarding the aircraft – so much

so that men were dropping like flies from heat exhaustion. I thought for a while that I might be a heat casualty but managed to hang on. My exit out of the door was a poor one causing many twists in my risers. After bicycling the twists out, it was already time to prepare to land. I hit hard and did the worst PLF I've ever done, but at least I wasn't hurt.

Lieutenant Bruce Woodgate

Later that year (1978), I participated in a weekend drill with the National Guard on August 12-13th. During the drill our unit visited the National Guard Armory in Hillsboro, Texas. One of my fellow soldiers in the 143d Airborne, Lieutenant Bruce Woodgate, also attended seminary with me in Fort Worth. Woodgate had trained and qualified as an Airborne Ranger, and I enjoyed serving under his command.

On Saturday night at the armory in Hillsboro, Woodgate and I witnessed to another guardsman about our faith in Jesus Christ. While we talked someone threw a tear gas grenade near us. As I explained in my journal the next day, "The gas got most of the Arlington guys who were inside the armory. I got a small taste of it myself."

Jump #10

Later that same month (August) I made my tenth jump. Pam planned to drive to Redbird Drop Zone in Dallas to watch it.

In my journal I described the jump as follows:

> On the 26th (last Saturday) I made my tenth jump. It was from a CH-47 Chinook and was my first Texas jump. The altitude was 1500 feet, which allowed me plenty of time to take some good pictures – my first from the air. It was a marvelous jump. Pam showed up too late to see me jump but she did see others jump.

As mentioned in my journal, during my tenth jump I took photographs for the first time while actually riding a parachute. I photographed a couple of other jumpers and I photographed the ground below. The picture I like the most shows my jump boots in contrast to the ground. In order to include my boots I had to lean forward over my reserve parachute, and a portion of the reserve chute made it into the photograph.

Figure 123 The author photographed his jump boots during a jump from a CH-47 Chinook helicopter over Redbird Drop Zone in Dallas, Texas (August 26, 1978).

Jump #11

Almost two months later, on Saturday, October 21st, I jumped again. The next day I wrote the following account of the experience:

Made my eleventh jump yesterday. It was from a C-130 Hercules. The DZ was at Fort Hood, consisting of rolling hills, ravines, rocks, and a few scattered trees. Like most everyone else who jumped, I hit like a sack of cement – hard!!! Injuries were numerous. Our CO separated his shoulder and our Safety Officer broke his leg. Many jumpers received cuts and abrasions from being dragged by 10-knot winds. I did a left front PLF that left the whole left side of my body in pain, but my hurt was minor compared to many of the others.

After the jump we hiked several miles through rugged terrain. C-130's then flew us back to Dallas.

The following month our unit returned to Fort Hood for live-fire training exercises, but a planned jump was cancelled because of rain.

Serving with Rick Warren

During seminary Pam and I belonged to Southcliff Baptist Church in Fort Worth. I served there as a Sunday school teacher in the Seminary Sunday School Department. The director of the department, Rick Warren, during the opening assemblies, gave some of the best devotions I've ever heard. Afterwards those of us who served under Rick's leadership would break up into smaller groups for Bible Study.

Rick Warren sometimes invited members of our department over to his house for Sunday school fellowships, and I enjoyed those times. He impressed me as a committed follower of Jesus Christ who truly cared about the needs of people. Rick later became famous for his ministry as founder and pastor of Saddleback Church in California and for his bestselling book, *The Purpose Driven Life*.[1] The book by George Mair about

---

[1] Rick Warren, *The Purpose Driven Life* (Grand Rapids, Michigan: Zondervan, 2002).

Warren's life called *A Life with Purpose*, on the front cover describes Warren as "The Most Inspiring Pastor of Our Time."[2]

Influence of Oscar Thompson

Another person whom God used to help me spiritually, Oscar Thompson, taught a class on personal evangelism and wrote a book called, *Concentric Circles of Concern* (published by his wife, Carolyn, after his death).[3] During my time in his class, he lived with multiple miloma – a deadly form of cancer that eventually took his life.

Oscar Thompson, more than anyone else, helped me understand the importance of building good relationships with people as a way of sharing Christ's love with them. And I found Oscar's insights quite helpful as I served the Lord in the Texas Army National Guard.

On one occasion a fellow member of my unit asked me to preach his wedding, but he didn't want a church wedding. Instead, he wanted me to perform the wedding ceremony in our National Guard Armory there in Arlington.

Due in part to Oscar Thompson's emphasis on building good relationships, I did the wedding at the armory. I guess that's about as close as I ever came to performing one of the official functions of a military chaplain in a military setting, and I did it as an Airborne Infantry soldier rather than as a chaplain.

---

[2] George Mair, *A Life with Purpose* (New York: Berkley Books, 2005).

[3] W. Oscar Thompson, *Concentric Circles of Concern* (Nashville, Tennessee: Broadman Press, 1981).

Leading Infantry Patrols

In January of 1979, my National Guard unit trained for riot control during one of our regular weekend drills. At that time I received word that I might get promoted to Buck Sergeant (E-5).

Then, in early February, I enjoyed some more infantry training. In my journal I later wrote, "Led my first infantry patrol Saturday. It was a fun experience since I didn't get lost."

Figure 124 Infantrymen of the 143d Airborne returning from a patrol at Fort Chaffee, Arkansas (Photo by author).

Jump #12

My 12th Jump probably took place at Fort Hood on March 10th or 11th, but I failed to write it down or wrote it down on a piece of note paper and then failed to add it to my journal. My journal for March 10—16 contains no entries at all, which probably means I was snowed under with school work at the seminary.

Unfortunately, I do not remember the details of that jump.

Jump #13

On Sunday, April 29th, I made the following entry in my journal:

> Made my third night jump last night. The jump was from a C-130. The drop zone was called Antelope. I made my worse landing yet and nearly broke my left leg. Fortunately I was able to walk away after lying on my back for a few minutes and allowing the pain to subside.

Because of the darkness and my inability of see a skyline marked by trees, I prepared to land prematurely. In Jump School the Black Hats taught me never to anticipate the ground too early as that causes the jumper to unconsciously reach for the ground with one or both of his legs. When I failed to make contact with the ground at the time I expected, I must have reached out unconsciously with my left leg.

Have you ever jammed a finger or a toe? Well, that's what I did to my leg – I straightened it out while reaching for the ground and hit stiff-legged. The pain that shot through my leg hurt like crazy, and I still don't know how I kept from breaking something.

Another paratrooper, Sergeant Gene Richardson, suffered a similar injury on that same jump. Apparently I made some moaning and groaning sounds as I laid there in pain because Gene said, "Monday, is that you?" I said, "Yes, is that you, Gene?" He replied, "Yes, it's me." And I said, "I think I may have broken my leg." Gene replied, "I think I may have broken my leg, too."

When we both walked off of the drop zone that night, we marveled over the fact that our legs still worked.

Jumps #14 & 15

My next two jumps took place during June of 1979. As explained in my journal entry for July 1st:

> Returned yesterday from two weeks of summer training with the Texas Army National Guard. It was a rough two weeks but the training was considerably better this year than it was last year. I made two more jumps – one from a CH-47 helicopter and one from a C-141 Starlifter, bringing my total number of jumps to 15.

Jumps #16 & 17

On Saturday, September 8, 1979, I did some more jumping with the 143d Airborne Infantry. Later that same day I made the following entry in my journal:

> Instead of jumping once, I jumped twice this morning, both jumps being from a CH-47 Chinook helicopter. On the first jump I had to slip away from two different jumpers plus was barely able to miss a paved road or the trees that lined both sides of that road. The second jump was eventful too as I had to slip away from the same jumper three different times because we kept drifting together. Both jumps were in Dallas at Redbird Drop Zone. My total number of jumps now is seventeen.

Jump #18

In early November of 1979 I jumped again. Following is the entry from my journal dated Wednesday, November 7th:

> Sunday morning I made my 18th jump. It was from 2500 feet and was out of a CH-47 helicopter. The parachute was a Dash-1, a modified T-10 that is steerable and has a 6 mph forward speed. I instantly fell in love with the parachute and would much prefer it over the T-10. I made the jump at Fort Hood on Rapedo Drop Zone.

Bad News for a Paratrooper

On January 14, 1980, my journal reads: "At drill yesterday I learned that our National Guard unit may soon be changed from an Airborne unit to a leg unit. Such an action would destroy both the morale and the enlistment efforts of our unit. . . . The thought saddens my heart."

In February I made the following entry in my journal:

> I have only two more National Guard drills left before I get out. If all goes well I'll get to make one more jump on my last drill.
>
> The rumors that our unit may cease to be Airborne have been confirmed. . . . It appears that my unit will become an Armored Cavalry unit.

On February 23 I wrote:

> The once I finish my next National Guard drill I won't have to sacrifice much-needed study time once a month to that job. Nonetheless, I'll miss the Guard in many ways. There is more of a military bent in me than I once thought. I'm also an adventurer who likes to face danger from time to time.

If I wanted danger, I'd get a good dose of it in less than a month when I made my last and most exciting jump, but I'll save that story for another chapter.

Figure 125 A C-130 drops paratroopers of the 143d Airborne Infantry (Photo by author).

Figure 126 Paratroopers of the 143d Airborne Infantry complete another jump (Photo by author).

Figure 127 Paratroopers of the 143d Airborne Infantry waiting to board a C-141 Starlifter (Photo by author).

Figure 128 Travis Monday (standing) waits to board a C-141 for a jump (Author's collection).

Figure 129 A C-141 Starlifter drops paratroopers of the 143ᵈ Airborne Infantry (Photo by author).

Figure 130 Travis Monday, a jet-jumpin' paratrooper after jumping from a C-141 Starlifter (Author's collection).

Figure 131 Seminary student and paratrooper Travis Monday in a UH-1B helicopter over Fort Chaffee, Arkansas (Author's collection).

Figure 132 The author in a rubber raft while doing a river crossing in Arkansas (Author's collection).

After Airborne

> Puppy sleeping on the floor,
> you cannot know my mind;
> you feel the carpet
> but cannot see
> Vietnam inside of me.
> I know I know the ghost of war.
> --Travis Monday

After I left the Texas Army National Guard, I graduated with a Master of Divinity degree from Southwestern Baptist Theological Seminary in Fort Worth, Texas.

Figure 133 The author receiving his Master of Divinity degree from Southwestern Baptist Theological Seminary in Fort Worth, Texas, from seminary president Russell Dilday (Author's collection).

Birth of Tim Monday

Pam added to the excitement of graduation week by giving birth to our first child, Timothy William Monday, during December of 1981.

I cannot possibly explain how happy I felt when a nurse at Fort Worth's Harris Hospital handed Tim to me right after the doctor extracted him from Pam's body by C-Section. Because of the longer recovery time that resulted from the C-Section, Pam did not get to attend my graduation ceremony at Travis Avenue Baptist Church.

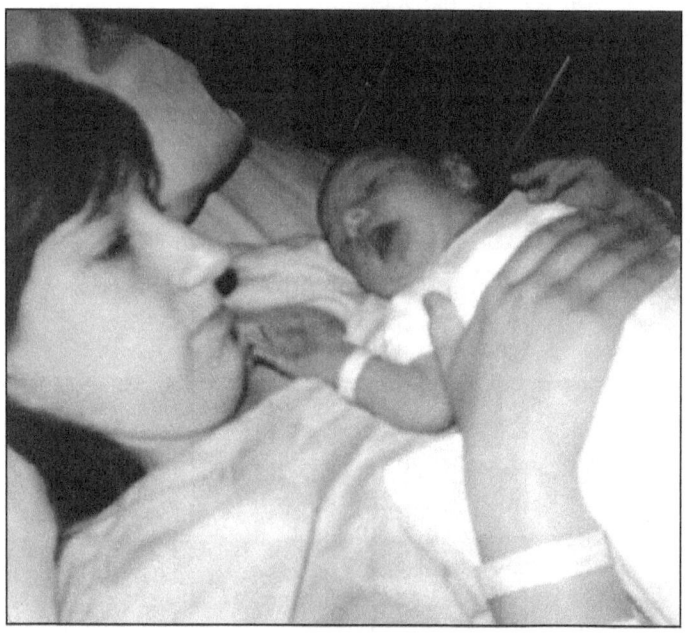

Figure 134 Pam Monday in Harris Hospital in Fort Worth, Texas, with her newborn son, Timothy William Monday (Photo by author; December, 1981).

Move to Yuba, Oklahoma

Pam, Tim, and I moved to Yuba, Oklahoma, during late summer in 1981. There I served as pastor of Yuba Baptist Church for almost 4 years.

On Sunday, August 1, 1982, I preached my first sermon as pastor of Yuba Baptist Church.

On August 5th I wrote in my journal:

> I am now "on the field" in Yuba, Oklahoma. Moving has been difficult and the process of unpacking is not yet completed. Amidst the chaos and confusion, I had my first deacons meeting and my first business meeting as a pastor. Through everything, the physical exhaustion included, God has been faithful to provide helpful neighbors, good health, and spiritual strength. Pam has been wonderful through the difficulty of moving and of leaving dear friends. I am thankful to be serving the living God.

The people of Yuba, Oklahoma, and the surrounding communities, were kind to us, and our next door neighbors, the Alexanders (Hall, Evelyn, Jeff, and Natalie), soon became trusted friends. Tim spent many hours at their house, and Evelyn and Natalie provided him with many glasses of chocolate milk.

Ordination to the Gospel Ministry

Although I had been a licensed minister for many years when I began serving as pastor of Yuba Baptist Church, I was not yet ordained. From the time that I accepted the call to become the pastor, I understood that the church would ordain me soon after I began serving.

On August 23, 1982, I met with the Director of Missions of Bryan Baptist Association, Rev. Carrell Hooper, to discuss my planned ordination. I also called my brother, Derrell, and asked him to preach my ordination sermon. Derrell accepted my invitation and later preached a powerful ordination message.

Yuba Baptist Church officially ordained me to the Gospel Ministry on September 19, 1982. Although I've never felt worthy of such a high calling, I cannot thank the Lord enough for allowing me to serve him all of these years through my preaching, teaching, and writing.

Figure 135 Left to Right: Rev. Carrell Hooper, Travis Monday, Pam Monday, and Tim Monday in Yuba Baptist Church in Yuba, Oklahoma, on the day of Travis' ordination to the Gospel Ministry (Author's collection).

PTSD-Related Depression in Yuba

The low point of my years in Yuba came in the form of a severe depression. A teenage boy whom I had befriended died in an accident, and I preached his funeral. Afterwards I struggled with depression for about three months.

By the grace of God, I still fulfilled my duties as pastor, and no one but Pam knew how depressed I felt. But the emotional pain I felt overwhelmed me at times and I could not figure out why the depression had hit me so hard. I later became convinced that the depression resulted from Post Traumatic Stress Disorder (PTSD) related to my Vietnam experience. The death of the young boy and preaching his funeral had triggered unresolved emotional trauma caused by the war.

Finally the depression began to disappear and I regained my sense of excitement about serving the Lord.

Birth of Jared Monday

One of the high points of my time in Yuba came with the birth of our second son, Jared Daniel Monday, in Texoma Medical Center in Denison, Texas, in May of 1984. As with Tim's birth, Jared's birth also filled my heart with joy. God had blessed us with two healthy sons.

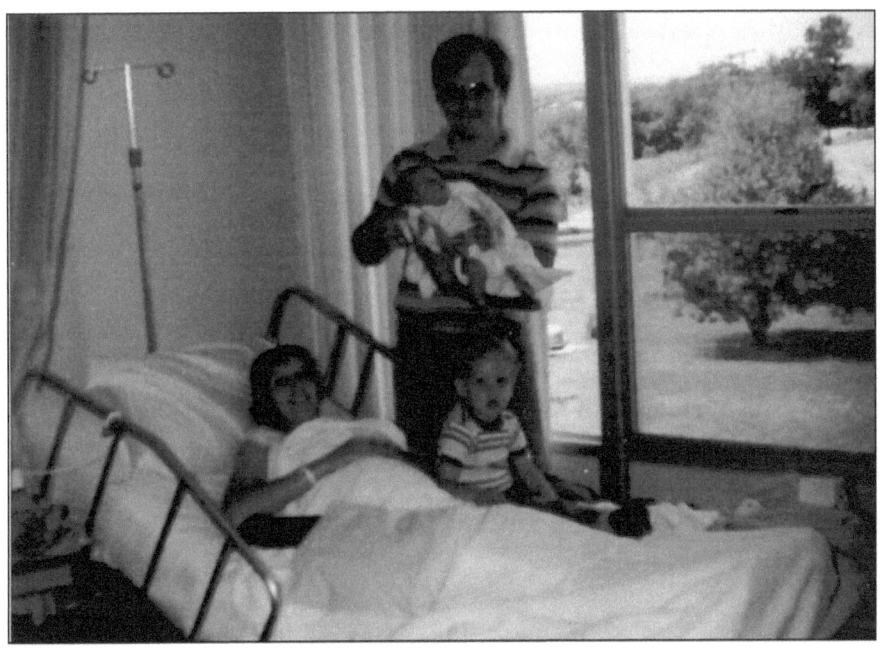

Figure 136 Travis, Pam, Tim, and Jared Monday at Texoma Medical Center in Denison, Texas, shortly after Jared's birth (Author's collection).

Move to Colorado City, Texas

In May of 1986, our family moved from Yuba, Oklahoma, to Colorado City, Texas. And on May 25, 1986, I preached my first message as pastor of Calvary Baptist Church.

I enjoyed most of my time in Colorado City, but Pam and I both faced times of great difficulty. She began having problems with depression and I experienced more of the symptoms of PTSD. I am grateful to the members of Calvary Baptist Church for supporting us in both the good and the bad times.

PTSD in Colorado City

My PTSD hit me numerous times and in different ways during my 10 ½ years in Colorado City. For example, as I officiated at numerous funerals, including the graveside portions of the services, I began feeling sad and depressed when I saw U.S. flags on graves at the cemeteries. While a certain amount of such feelings might be viewed as "normal," the intensity and frequency convinced me that something about my experience required attention. For a time this problem grew progressively worse and I prayed many times that God would help me overcome it.

I also began having nightmares about Vietnam. One night I dreamed that I was in Vietnam and that I could hear a Viet Cong soldier running at me from behind, and somehow I knew he intended to kill me. At the last possible second, I turned around and kicked him.

When I woke up I heard Pam screaming, "You kicked me! You kicked me! Why did you kick me?" Fortunately the covers and my position in the bed kept me from causing her serious injury, but we both felt unnerved by the experience. And that same sort of thing happened repeatedly.

These PTSD problems and others caused me to pray for God to guide me to whatever resources I might need. He answered those prayers, in part, through another Vietnam veteran by the name of Chuck Dean.

Chuck Dean and Point Man Ministries

Somehow I learned of a ministry called Point Man, and I got access to a copy of their publication *Reveille*. After discovering that the ministry consisted of Vietnam veterans helping other Vietnam veterans find God's help for their PTSD, I believed that God had answered my prayers.

On February 23, 1989, I received a copy of a book by Chuck Dean, the leader of Point Man Ministries, called *Nam Vet: Making Peace with Your Past*. By the time I completed my first reading of *Nam Vet*, I could sense God using it to bring strength and healing into my life. The Lord used the book to help me better understand my struggle with PTSD.

For example, as I reflected back on the depression that clobbered me in Yuba, Oklahoma, after preaching the funeral of a young boy, God used Dean's book to help me better understand the concept of "triggers." In his book he explains them as follows:

> *Trigger* is the term used to describe those events and reminders that cause veterans and other trauma victims to respond adversely because of their past experiences. When a particular traumatic incident occurs, it is imprinted and stored permanently in the mind. What makes these subconscious memories especially harmful is that they continue to cause stressful and inappropriate reactions when stimulated by triggers in our present environment.[1]

The death and funeral of that teenage boy triggered my unresolved feelings about the young girl I saw in Vietnam whom had been blown up by Viet Cong hand grenades. At the time of the incident I had stuffed my feelings deep inside. Later, in Yuba, preaching that funeral allowed those feelings to emerge and overwhelm me, especially when combined with the "normal" feelings of grief I felt over the death of my young friend.

---

[1] Chuck Dean, *Nam Vet: Making Peace with Your Past* (United States of America: WordSmith Publishing, 2000), 149.

Earlier, while working as a surgical orderly at Hendricks Medical Center in Abilene, Texas, seeing skin grafts performed on a young burn victim also had served as a trigger for those powerful feelings.

Before long I sensed that God not only wanted to help me through Point Man Ministries and through Dean's book *Nam Vet*, but he also wanted me to get involved in Point Man as an outpost leader. With the Lord's help and the assistance of some other Vietnam veterans in my church, I served as an outpost leader for two years before sensing God's leadership to help my fellow veterans in other ways.

Figure 137 **The author's ministry card as an Outpost Director of Point Man International Ministries (Author's collection).**

Doug Greer, who served in Vietnam with the Marines for 39 months before coming home wounded, helped me reach out to other Vietnam veterans. Tom Kelly, a school teacher in one of Colorado City's schools, served in Vietnam, and he, too, helped me minister to other Vietnam veterans. Another church member, Ronnie Blair, also served in the Vietnam War.

Patriotic Parade in Colorado City

As the result of a new wave of patriotism related to Operation Desert Shield and Operation Desert Storm during our nation's first war in Iraq, the people of Colorado City decided to honor our military personnel by having a parade, and some of us who had served in Vietnam accepted an invitation to ride on a float.

On July 5, 1991, I reflected on that experience by making the following entry in my journal:

> On July 4, 1971, I was serving in the former Republic of South Vietnam. On July 4, 1991 – twenty years later – I finally got my parade. While not wanting to make it sound like getting a parade was all that important to me, I must acknowledge that it felt good to experience it.

Figure 138 Travis Monday (center) with Tom Kelly (far left) and Doug Greer (far right) in a parade honoring U. S. military personnel and veterans in Colorado City, Texas (Author's collection; July 4, 1991).

It was particularly moving for me to see Tom Kelly carrying a framed copy of the name of a friend of his who was killed in Vietnam . . . .[2]

Speaking at Colorado Middle School

About a year before I left Colorado City, I received an invitation to speak at the Colorado Middle School where our son, Tim, attended classes. In fact, Tim introduced me in a school assembly on November 10, 1995.

The school administration wanted me to speak on the theme, "What It Means to Be a Veteran," and I had 3 to 4 minutes to do it. Here is what I said:

What It Means to Be a Veteran

I've been asked to speak briefly to you about what it means to be a veteran. As I begin, I want you to understand a few things about my background. I'm not a hero but I have been in a war – the Vietnam War. I haven't fought in any big battles but I have been shot at and I have fired some shots. I haven't seen battlefields covered with bodies but I have seen a child who was blown-up by the grenades of Viet Cong guerillas. I've never ridden aircraft or ships into a raging battle but I have parachuted out of airplanes and helicopters. Most of all, I have been in the U.S. military in service of my country.

My feelings about being a veteran cannot be separated from my feelings about our flag. While I was in the 5th grade in Floydada, Texas, I wrote the following words about the flag:

---

[2] Lonnie Lloyd of Kansas City, Kansas, who grew up with Tom Kelly, died in an ambush in Vietnam at the age of 19 years while serving with the U. S. Marines. Kelly carried a framed copy of his name in order to honor Lonnie Lloyd's memory.

The flag when it is unfurled makes me think of the wars of the United States of America. And the men who gave their lives for our country.

It makes me feel proud. I can't really put my feelings in words. It is kind of a good warm feeling right down in my heart.

I think of the states the flag's stars stand for.

I think of the other countries that fought on our side.

I think of all the colonies and people in them. And all their troubles that they went through just to settle the United States of America.

I think of America our great nation. Our free country. I think of freedom, justice and liberty. The land of the free. And the home of the brave.

These feelings that I expressed as a 5th grader are still true today.

What else does it mean for me to be veteran? To me being a veteran means . . .

. . . loving our country and loving our flag.

. . . sharing a special kinship with all other veterans.

. . . realizing, in the words of Billy Ray Cyrus, that "all gave some – some gave all. Some stood through for the red, white, and blue; some had to fall."

. . . it means remembering those who had to fall – including my old friend Steve Seigler.

. . . it means remembering a puppy named Mickey who shared my war – and died while still a puppy.

. . . it means spending Christmas without walking for miles with an M-60 machine gun on my shoulder.

. . . it means loving and enjoying my family – a privilege many others never got to experience.

. . . it means replacing the oft-spoken words of that war – "It don't mean nothin'!" with the words, "Life *does* mean something!"

. . . it means taking advantage of my God-given opportunities as a survivor to help make this world better for my children and grandchildren.

. . . it means striving to make America one nation, under God, indivisible, with liberty and justice for all.

I close quickly and simply with these words: "God bless you and God bless America!"

Pam and Jared also attended the school assembly, and having them and Tim there made the event more meaningful.

More Seminary Studies

The members of Calvary Baptist Church in Colorado City treated my family and I quite well. They even allowed me to return to Southwestern Baptist Theological Seminary to work on a Doctor of Ministry degree. I received that degree in December of 1989 – the birth month of both my brother Derrell and my son Tim.

Other Veterans in Colorado City

My love and appreciation for veterans is not limited to Vietnam veterans – I respect and admire veterans of other wars also. Two World War II veterans who became my good friends in Colorado City were T. J. Geiger and Edward Roach – both of whom served the Lord with me as members of Calvary Baptist Church.

Move to Sweetwater, Texas

In November of 1996, about ten and a half years since my arrival in Colorado City, my family and I moved to Sweetwater, Texas, where I began serving as pastor of Trinity Baptist Church. I would continue there in Sweetwater for five and a half years, and during that time I continued to work on my own PTSD while attempting to help other Vietnam veterans with theirs. But my involvement with veterans of other wars also increased. I found myself preaching the funerals of more and more World War II veterans.

Something else that continued in Sweetwater was my interest in parachutes and the people who used them. Although I did not choose to jump again, I began gathering stories of other jumpers and their experiences. I wanted to learn more about the history of parachuting.

Parachute Jumps of President George H. W. Bush

One day while visiting church members at Hendricks Medical Center in Abilene, Texas, I noticed security men in suits positioning themselves throughout the hospital. When I asked someone what was going on, he said, "Governor Bush is about to speak here in the hospital."

Figure 139 Former President George H. W. Bush made several parachute jumps, including 2 jumps on his 80th birthday.

Although I had not known about the Governor's planned speech when I arrived, I decided to go hear him speak. By that time I knew that his father, President George H. W. Bush had made an emergency parachute jump during World War II while serving as a fighter pilot. He had made another jump the day before his son Governor Bush arrived in Abilene at the hospital. So I heard Governor Bush make some humorous remarks about his father's adventure. President George H. W. Bush later made two more parachute jumps on his 80th birthday.

Rigdon Edwards, Bennet Monde, and the WASP

While serving as pastor of Trinity Baptist Church of Sweetwater, I joined the local Rotary Club, where I soon met Rigdon Edwards, a former flight instructor for the Women Airforce Service Pilots (WASP) of World War II at Sweetwater's Avenger Field. His stories about the WASP got me thinking about writing an article on these aviation pioneers and their parachutes.

Figure 140 Rigdon Edwards helped the author learn about the Women Airforce Service Pilots (WASP) of World War II. He was one of their flight instructors at Avenger Field (Courtesy of the Pioneer Museum in Sweetwater, Texas).

Major Bennet B. Monde, author of the book *Wings Over Sweetwater* and former commander of Avenger Field, added to my knowledge of the WASP.

When the WASP returned to Sweetwater in the year 2000 for a WASP reunion, I interviewed some of them about their experiences with parachutes. The editor of the *Sweetwater Reporter* published the story in the newspaper. I had written other stories for the *Sweetwater Reporter* as a part of my volunteer work for the Pioneer Museum in Sweetwater. Museum Director Franzas Cupp had set up a WASP Room in the museum where I did additional research. She, too, had urged me to write about the WASP.

Parachutes & Prayer (WASP Lorraine Zillner Rodgers)

Figure 141 WASP Lorraine Zillner Rodgers at the WASP 2000 Reunion in Sweetwater, Texas. She made an emergency parachute jump while in training at Avenger Field (Photo by author; October 5, 2000).

Of all the WASP I interviewed about their parachutes, Lorraine Zillner Rodgers gave me the best story. While training at Avenger Field in Sweetwater, she jumped from a Vultee BT-13.[3] Because of her closeness to the ground, she pulled her ripcord early. "Instead of counting to 10, I counted 1, 2, 10, and pulled my ripcord, and my chute opened, and I touched the ground," she said. In other words, the shorter count saved her life.

But Rodgers believes that she survived her emergency bail-out for another reason. When questioned by an investigative board about her jump from the aircraft, she sensed the skepticism of her questioners. She

---

[3] Some sources say that Lorraine Zillner Rodgers jumped from a BT-15 rather than a BT-13. These two aircraft are almost identical.

had bailed out of an airplane in an inverted spin, which aviators of that day viewed as impossible. When pressed for a fuller explanation of how she did it, she did a little questioning of her own. She asked, "Have you ever heard of prayer?" When I interviewed her many years later, Lorraine Zillner Rodgers still believed in both parachutes and prayer.

September 11, 2001

Figure 142 Sweetwater, Texas, Mayor Jay Lawrence greeted the author at a meeting of the City Commissioners on the morning of the September 11, 2001, attacks against America. Lawrence wanted the author to include the unfolding situation in his prayer before the Commission (Photo by author).

Almost a year after my interview with Rodgers during WASP 2000, America suffered a series of attacks by terrorists. On the morning of September 11, 2001, while preparing to leave the house to say a prayer at the meeting of the Sweetwater City Commission, I witnessed on television the terrorist attacks on the World Trade Center. When I arrived at City Hall, Sweetwater Mayor Jay Lawrence greeted me and asked if I knew what had happened. I answered that I did and that I intended to mention the situation in my prayer, and he said, "Good!"

I don't remember what all I said, but I do remember praying for the families of those who died and for anyone trapped in the wreckage and in need of rescue. I also prayed for wisdom for the leaders of our nation. As terrorists continue to threaten freedom-loving people throughout the world, I continue to pray for our leaders. I also pray for our men and women in uniform wherever they serve.

Move to San Angelo, Texas

By the time of the first anniversary of 9-11, Pam and I had relocated to San Angelo, Texas, where I had begun serving as pastor of Harris Avenue Baptist Church.

Soon after I arrived in San Angelo, I discovered that the city and the surrounding area served as the home base for a good number of writers, including the western novelist, Elmer Kelton; novelist, Ken Hodgson; novelist, Ken Casper; novelist, Barbara Jennison; newspaper columnist and non-fiction book writer, Ross McSwain; regional historian, Barbara Barton; non-fiction writer, Wanda Langley; novelist, Dave Gottshall; non-fiction writer and newspaper columnist, Russell S. Smith; non-fiction writer and newspaper columnist, Judy Niemann; fiction and non-fiction writer Dr. Pres Darby; and writer and minister Dr. W. E. ("Bill") Thorn.

In San Angelo I met and befriended numerous veterans of the Vietnam War and other wars, and I continued preaching funerals for World War II veterans and for veterans of other wars.

Remembering Steve Seigler

As pastor of Harris Avenue Baptist Church in San Angelo, I wrote weekly articles for the church newsletter. As we approached another Memorial Day, I wrote the following article, dated May 19, 2003:

> Memorial Day is a day for remembering those men and women who have made the ultimate sacrifice for our nation.
>
> How can we properly observe Memorial Day? We can observe it by visiting cemeteries and placing flags or flowers on the graves of our fallen heroes. We can observe it by visiting memorials and by flying the U.S. Flag at half-staff until noon. We can participate in a National Moment of Remembrance at 3:00 p.m. – a time in which it is appropriate for "Taps" to be played. We also may observe it by renewing a pledge to aid the widows, widowers, and orphans of our fallen dead, and to aid disabled veterans.
>
> Memorial Day always reminds me of Steve Seigler, who, like me, graduated from Plainview High School in Plainview, Texas, then joined the U. S. Army. I still remember talking with Steve during his leave just before he left for Vietnam. By the time I came home for leave before I went to Vietnam, I had learned that Steve had been killed in Vietnam.
>
> Since that time, I've made many visits to Steve's grave, and I always think about the fact that he never had the opportunity to get married and raise children, yet the Lord has allowed me to do both.
>
> Let's not forget those who gave their lives for our freedom.

Shortly after this article appeared in our church newsletter, someone from the *San Angelo Standard-Times* called and asked to interview me about Steve Seigler. I agreed to do the interview. A staff writer for the *San Angelo Standard-Times*, Joshua Parrott, interviewed me in my home on May 23rd. Instead of publishing Parrott's article on or near Memorial Day, as originally planned, the paper released it on July 5, 2003, in connection with Independence Day. Somehow word of the article reached some of Steve Seigler's family in Plainview, and I soon received a message of appreciation from Steve's sister, Brooks Seigler Price.

Between the time I wrote the article mentioning Steve Seigler for the church newsletter, and the time the newspaper released Parrott's article, I did more research on Steve Seigler and succeeded in making contact with

John Nichols of California, who flew with Steve on the day of his death. Nichols, who shares my desire to honor Steve's memory, sent me the photos of Steve in Vietnam that appear in this book.

W. F. Matthews and the Lost Battalion

While serving as pastor of Harris Avenue Baptist Church in San Angelo, I learned that one of our deacons, W. F. Matthews, had survived 3 ½ years as a prisoner of war of the Japanese during World War II. When he told me that he regretted not writing about his P.O.W. experiences, I said, "Maybe we can do something about that."

Figure 143 Former World War II prisoner-of-war W. F. Matthews with his wife, Gladys, in San Angelo, Texas (Photo by author; November 11, 2006).

Over a period of about 2 years, we did do something about it – we put his story into a book and called it *W. F. Matthews: Lost Battalion Survivor*. Writing this true story of combat and captivity strengthened me in my own walk with the Lord and helped me develop as a writer. Reliving his experiences with him also helped me with my own PTSD.

A short time later, the Lord blessed me even more by allowing me to introduce W. F. for induction into the Southwest Military Museum Hall of Fame in San Angelo. I introduced him on the evening of November 13, 2004. During the ceremony, held at the San Angelo Museum of Fine Arts, I had the honor of reading the letter of nomination I had written in behalf of Matthews. Afterwards I said, "It is a great honor for me to present to you a real American hero – W. F. Matthews!" The crowd responded with a standing ovation.

The Otto Carter Story

Figure 144 Otto Carter, Jr., with one of his two P-47 Thunderbolts named "Sweetwater Swatter" (Courtesy of Otto Carter, III).

Before I met Matthews and before I left Sweetwater to move to San Angelo, I noticed a photograph in the Pioneer Museum of a man named Otto Carter standing beside a P-47 Thunderbolt airplane. On the side of the fuselage someone had painted the words, "Sweetwater Swatter." I left

Sweetwater regretting that I had not researched the story behind the photo. I even prayed, "Lord, I'd sure appreciate it if you would allow me to write about Otto Carter some day."

A few years later the Lord let me write "The Otto Carter Story" with the help of Carter's son, Otto Carter, III, and his widow, Lillian Carter. They let me interview them and also loaned me audio cassette tapes of an interview by Otto Carter, III, with his father. Otto Carter, Jr., had died before I had a chance to meet him. Soon after his return from World War II, he had made an emergency parachute jump out of a P-47 near the town of Merkel, Texas. I included "The Otto Carter Story" in a book of World War II aviation history stories entitled, *Wings, WASP, & Warriors*.

The Moving Wall at Angelo State University

On November 8, 2002, while living in San Angelo, I visited a portable version of the Vietnam War Memorial for the second time. When my secretary/receptionist from Harris Avenue Baptist Church, Colleen Heath, told me that I could visit the Moving Wall on the campus of Angelo State University (ASU), I knew wanted to see it.

During the visit I photographed the names of Steven Seigler and Jimmy Awalt – both from Plainview, Texas. I had found their names once before when I visited the Moving Wall on the campus of McMurray University in Abilene, but at that time I did not have a camera with me.

The man who helped me find the names on the wall in San Angelo, Jim Edwards, told me that he was the current president of the Concho Valley Vietnam Veterans of America, Chapter 457. This organization had arranged for the Moving Wall to visit San Angelo. On a previous occasion VVA 457 had arranged a visit of the Moving Wall at San Angelo's Goodfellow Air Force Base.

Vietnam Veterans of America, Chapter 457

In order to learn more about the history of VVA 457, I interviewed one of its founders and former presidents, Armando Vasquez, on November 10, 2005. Vasquez served with the Army's 75th Airborne Rangers in Vietnam in 1971. After he suffered shrapnel wounds from a mortar round explosion, he received a medical discharge in February of 1972.

Figure 145 Vietnam veteran Armando Vasquez of San Angelo, Texas, helped start Vietnam Veterans of America, Chapter 457 (Photo by author; November 11, 2005).

In 1988, Vasquez and fellow Vietnam veteran Tom Bright, while serving as police officers in San Angelo, visited the Moving Wall in Big Spring, Texas. Their visit stirred up some powerful emotions and they felt deeply moved by the experience. According to Vasquez, "Some people say it's a healing wall; it took a long time for that to come around. It was a very painful experience for both of us."

Later that same year, on Memorial Day, Vasquez and Bright attended a ceremony at the Tom Green County Courthouse. An encounter there with other Vietnam veterans resulted in an intense time of tears and embracing.

This group of Vietnam veterans watched different organizations place wreaths in memory of fallen comrades. As Vasquez later told me, "Not one wreath was placed for those who died in Vietnam." Vasquez, Bright, and some other Vietnam veterans made up their minds to do something about it.

Figure 146 Tom Bright joined with Armando Vasquez to help start Concho Valley Vietnam Veterans in San Angelo, Texas (Photo by author; May 30, 2005).

With the help of Alberto Rodriquez of Kerrville, Texas, a small group of Vietnam veterans started an organization in San Angelo called Concho Valley Vietnam Veterans. A short time later they became affiliated with a national organization known as Vietnam Veterans of America (VVA). The original founders of the group included Armando Vasquez, Herschel Carmichael, Tom Bright, Tom Davis, and others.

Figure 147 Alberto Rodriguez Hall in San Angelo, Texas, serves as the meeting place for Vietnam Veterans of America, Chapter 457 (Photo by author; July 10, 2004).

Concho Valley Vietnam Veterans Memorial

When I learned from the *San Angelo Standard-Times* of a Memorial Day ceremony scheduled for May 31, 2004, out at the local airport, I decided to attend. Later that same day I made the following entry in my journal:

> At 2:00 p.m. today I attended a Memorial Day ceremony at the Vietnam War Memorial at Mathis Field. The event was well attended and I took advantage of the opportunity to take a large number of photos of both the memorial and the people there for the ceremony.

The Vietnam veterans responsible for the program impressed me by honoring veterans of other wars – not just Vietnam veterans. In fact, that day they honored a young Marine by the name of Elias Torres, III, who had recently died in Iraq.

Figure 148 Paver placed at the Concho Valley Vietnam Veterans Memorial in honor of Elias Torrez, III, who died in action in Iraq (Photo by author).

Before I left the Memorial, Jerry Flowers invited me to join the local chapter of Vietnam Veterans of America (VVA).

Figure 149 Vietnam veteran Jerry Flowers invited the author to join Vietnam Veterans of America, Chapter 457 (Photo by author; November 11, 2004).

Later I researched the history of the Concho Valley Vietnam Veterans Memorial. Herschel Carmichael told me how he and some other members of the VVA 457 decided they wanted a permanent Vietnam War memorial for San Angelo and the surrounding area. They agreed to use a Huey helicopter as the centerpiece for the memorial.

"So we went through Robert Junell, our representative for this area, to see if he could get us a Huey helicopter, which he did," explained Carmichael.

The Huey, which came out of Fort Rucker, Alabama, had endured combat in Vietnam, even getting shot down once. The members of VVA 457 received it and placed it at the National Guard Armory on Highway 67 while they searched for a site for the Memorial.

Figure 150 Vietnam veteran Herschel Carmichael at the Concho Valley Vietnam Veterans Memorial at Mathis Field, San Angelo, Texas (Photo courtesy of Herschel Carmichael).

After a lot of hard work and lots of ups and downs, on May 17, 1997, the Concho Valley Vietnam Veterans Memorial was dedicated in connection with Armed Forces Day.

Visit by Vietnam Veteran Bob Dils

Bob Dils, my best friend in Vietnam during my time with D Company of the 69th Engineer Battalion, arrived in San Angelo to visit me on September 7, 2005. His timely visit allowed me to show him the Concho Valley Vietnam Veterans Memorial, and he connected with the Memorial immediately.

Dils' visit allowed me to interview him face-to-face about his memories of our time in Vietnam. We browsed through old photos and he helped me remember some things that helped me write this book.

Figure 151 Vietnam veteran Bob Dils (left) with Travis Monday in San Angelo, Texas (Author's collection; September, 2005).

Robert E. Dils, born in January of 1953 in Dayton, Ohio, joined the Army in August of 1970. He took Basic Combat Training at Fort Polk,

Louisiana. Like me, he took the Leadership Preparation Course at Fort Leonard Wood, Missouri, and then graduated from AIT there with the MOS of Heavy Equipment Repairman (62B20).

When I asked Dils what stood out in his memory about our days at Tan Hoa, he replied, "The brotherhood. We had nobody – we had nothing to depend on other than knowing that we were together and sharing literally everything."

Since Dils and I both had at times questioned the validity of the Vietnam War, I asked him how he felt at the time of the interview about serving in Vietnam. He gave me the following answer:

> Oh, absolutely proud to have served. Proud to have helped the people that we did with the roads and to do the job that we were called to do. Absolutely. And whether it would have been building the roads or some other assignment – absolutely proud.

And like me, Bob Dils is a Vietnam veteran who openly acknowledges his faith in Jesus Christ.

Southwest Military Museum

I've already mentioned the Southwest Military Museum in connection with the induction of W. F. Matthews into its Hall of Fame. The museum has since closed down, but it holds a special place in my heart.

In my journal for November 7, 2002, I made the following entry: "After lunch today I visited the Southwest Military Museum, which is a small museum that is just getting started. Right now they have a Vietnam War display to go along with the Vietnam Veterans Memorial Moving Wall that is at ASU."

During that visit I met one of the museum's founders, Robert Carmichael, a veteran of the Korean War. His brother, Vietnam veteran

Herschel Carmichael, at that time served as president of the museum, and I later interviewed Herschel about its history.

After joining the Army, Herschel Carmichael went through Basic Combat Training at Fort Bliss, Texas. He then took his Advanced Individual Training (AIT) at Fort Leonard Wood, Missouri, where he trained as a heavy equipment operator. He served in Vietnam with the 520th and 537th Personnel Service Company out of Bien Hoa from June 1969 to June 1970.

According to Herschel, plans for the Southwest Military Museum date back to 1993 or earlier, but it took a long time to find a site and to get the museum established. During my interview with Herschel he said: "Officially it opened in November of 2003 – I think that was the official date. Now, it opened up occasionally before that like when we had the Moving Wall here, when it opened up for a week. Vietnam Veterans of America helped donate money towards it -- $10,000."

VVA 457 Chaplain Roy Hansen

Figure 152 Vietnam veteran Roy Hansen served as chaplain of the Vietnam Veterans of America, Chapter 457 in San Angelo, Texas (Photo by author; November 11, 2004).

When I discovered that VVA 457 had a chaplain by the name of Roy Hansen, I made friends with him immediately. It didn't take me long to figure out that Hansen was a Vietnam veteran who loved other Vietnam veterans and who wanted to share his faith with them.

Hansen served in Vietnam with the Marines as a radio operator, and he saw lots of combat, including action at Khe Sanh in the 1967 Hill Fights that preceded the better known Siege of Khe Sanh in 1968. When I interviewed him in San Angelo on October 6, 2005, he explained, "Because Khe Sanh was inside of a bowl, you had to control the hills around it in order to control Khe Sanh. And those battles in 1967 were just totally vicious."

After Vietnam, Hansen spent a good number of years drinking and fighting. "I was so violent," he told me, "that I was excluded from certain bars and public places because I had been in so many fights and that kind of thing."

But in 1983 Hansen accepted Jesus Christ as his Lord and Savior, and his life changed completely. When Vietnam Veterans of America, Chapter 326 in Janesville, Wisconsin, chose him as their chaplain, their action made him the first Vietnam Veterans of America chaplain in the State of Wisconsin.

Hansen has since made 3 missionary trips to Vietnam with the group of Dave Roever out of Forth Worth, Texas. After moving to San Angelo, he became chaplain of Vietnam Veterans of America, Chapter 457, and that's how I met him. When he stepped down as chaplain after two years of service, the Vietnam veterans of VVA 457 made me their new chaplain, and I'm grateful for the honor of serving my fellow Vietnam veterans in this way.

Resurrection of San Angelo's Veterans Day Parade

After many years without a Veterans Day Parade in San Angelo, the All-Vets Council of San Angelo resurrected the event on November 11, 2004. Jim Edwards, a former president of VVA 457 and a member of the All-Vets Council, played a significant role in bringing back the Veterans Day Parade.

Figure 153 Vietnam veteran Jim Edwards is a former president of Vietnam Veterans of America, Chapter 457 (Photo by author; November 11, 2004).

As I understand it, before the parade of 2004, the last time the people of San Angelo had seen a Veterans Day Parade was in 1978. Although I could have ridden on a float with other Vietnam veterans in 2004, I chose instead to photograph the event as a spectator.

The following year on November 11, 2005, I chose to ride in the parade. Afterwards I made the following entry in my journal:

Much of this day was spent on Veterans Day activities with VVA Chapter 457. Last year I photographed the first Veterans Day Parade in San Angelo in many years. This year I rode with other Vietnam veterans on a flatbed trailer lined with metal folding chairs.

Since San Angelo schools let out for the parade this year, and perhaps for other reasons also, the crowds were much larger. I was pleasantly surprised at how many people applauded for our Vietnam veterans' group as we passed by and also at how frequently people would shout, "Thank You!" I was deeply touched by their expressions of gratitude.

As I rode along, I began to realize that I was not there primarily for my personal pleasure but rather to serve as a living reminder of all the men and women who served in that unpopular war -- especially those who died there.

I pray that the Lord will continue to use me and other Vietnam veterans as living reminders of those who served our nation in Vietnam. And after we've all died off, I pray that the people of our nation will always remember the price of freedom.

"Together in War – Together in Peace"

Figure 154 Vietnam veteran Tom Davis developed a logo for Vietnam Veterans of America, Chapter 457. The logo includes the words, "Together in War; Together in Peace" (Photo by author; May 30, 2005).

During the early days of VVA 457, Vietnam veteran Tom Davis developed a logo meant to represent the beliefs and values of the chapter. Included in the circular shaped design are the words, "Together in war; together in peace." That motto summarizes the feelings of brotherhood felt by many Vietnam veterans, including me.

Figure 155 San Angelo Vietnam veteran Tom Davis designed this logo for VVA 457 (Photo of logo by author).

Another Approach to Overcoming PTSD

As I have faced my own problems with PTSD and as I've attempted to help other war veterans with theirs, I've developed an alternative meaning for the letters PTSD. Instead of thinking of them as referring to Post

Traumatic Stress Disorder (PTSD), I use them to help me overcome that problem through faith in Jesus Christ. For me PTSD reminds me to Prevail Through Surrendering Daily (PTSD). Surrendering to whom? To the Lord Jesus Christ, and also to his will for my life.

Replace:

- P – *Post*
- T – *Traumatic*
- S – *Stress*
- D – *Disorder*

With:

- P -- *Prevail*
- T – *Through*
- S – *Surrendering*
- D -- *Daily*

I know that many veterans dislike the idea of surrendering to anyone, but I've learned that surrendering to the Lord every day increases my ability to face and overcome Post Traumatic Stress Disorder and anything else that life throws at me.

Figure 156 The Monday family in Colorado City, Texas (Author's collection).

Figure 157 Travis Monday with his son, Jared, at a veterans' event in Big Spring, Texas (Author's collection; October 7, 1990).

Figure 158 Vietnam veteran Travis Monday in his home in Colorado City, Texas, just before riding in a parade honoring military personnel and veterans (Author's collection; July 4, 1991).

Figure 159 A young girl, Emily Gannaway of Trinity Baptist Church in Sweetwater, Texas, gave this drawing to the author after church one day (Courtesy of Emily Gannaway).

Figure 160 Chief Master Sergeant James B. Heath left his mark at Goodfellow Air Force Base in San Angelo, Texas, and elsewhere, through his dedicated service in the U. S. Air Force (Photo courtesy of Colleen Heath).

Figure 161 Paver honoring James B. Heath placed at the Concho Valley Vietnam Memorial by his widow, Colleen Heath (Photo by author; Nov. 11, 2006).

Figure 162 Chaplain Travis Monday with Colleen Heath at the Concho Valley Vietnam Veterans Memorial in San Angelo, Texas (Photo by Pam Monday; November 11, 2006).

Figure 163 The Concho Valley Vietnam Veterans Memorial (Photo by author; May 30, 2005).

Adios Airborne

Figure 164 Cover of a small pamphlet given to Travis Monday while he served with the 143d Airborne Infantry in Arlington, Texas (Author's collection).

Perhaps you've wondered where I got the idea for the title of this book, *Nineteen Jumps and a Prayer*. By the time you finish reading this chapter, you will understand.

Figure 165 Airborne Infantry Sgt. Travis Monday at Redbird Drop Zone in Dallas, Texas, after jumping from a CH-47 Chinook helicopter (Author's collection; August 26, 1978).

From Airborne to Armored Cavalry

As mentioned previously, the members of the 143d Airborne Infantry of the Texas Army National Guard received word that our unit would soon change from an Airborne Infantry unit to an Armored Cavalry unit.

The new name for the unit became TRP I, 3d SQDN, 163d ARMD CAV REGT, so that is the name of the unit on my honorable discharge from the Texas Army National Guard. But I left the unit without any involvement whatsoever in its Armored Cavalry operations.

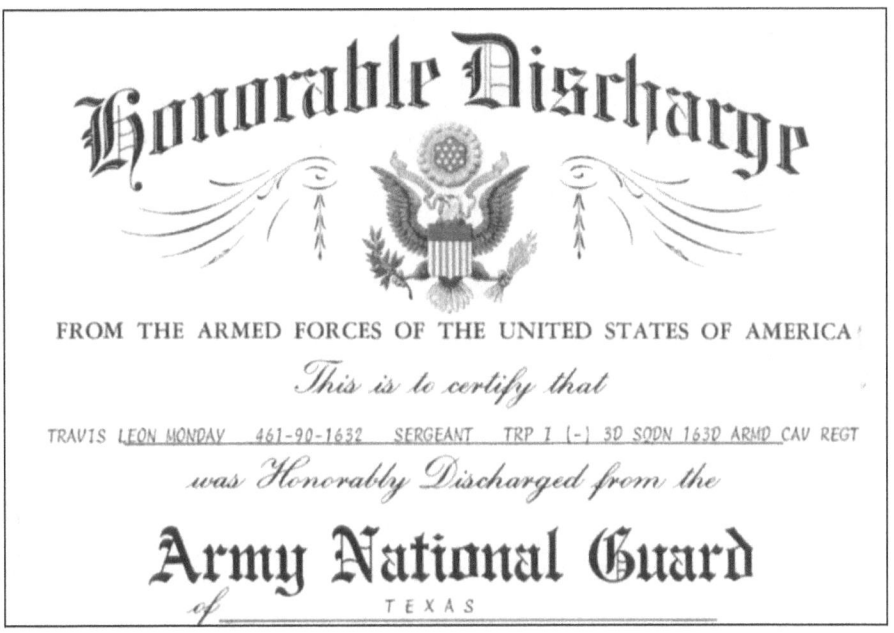

Figure 166 The author's discharge from the Texas Army National Guard makes it appear that he served in an Armored Cavalry unit, but he never actually received any Armored Cavalry training. The change in his unit from Airborne Infantry to Armored Cavalry came just as he was leaving the unit (Author's collection).

Last Day of Jumping for the 143d Airborne Infantry

Before the change to Armored Cavalry, our Airborne Infantry unit flew to Austin for one final day of parachute jumping.

Jump #19

During my 19th jump, I came face-to-face with death. As I descended toward the ground, the boots of another paratrooper plowed into my canopy and caused it to collapse. The collision occurred just as I was about to prepare to land, so I knew I would hit the ground before I could successfully deploy my reserve parachute. I expected to die.

As soon as I realized that I might die, I started praying. I asked the Lord to take care of my wife, Pam (before we had children), and I said, "Lord, here I come! My life is in Your hands."

Then, just as I was about to hit the ground, I felt a gentle but welcome tug – my main parachute had re-opened. By the grace of God I made a good landing and walked away without even a scratch or a bruise.

The Other Jumpin' Jesus

Earlier in this book I mentioned an Army chaplain at Fort Benning, Georgia, known by the nickname of "Jumpin' Jesus." He had earned this nickname by jumping with young soldiers when they made their first jump during Airborne School.

My last jump as an Army paratrooper helped me to view my Lord and Savior Jesus Christ as the real Jumpin' Jesus because he never forsakes us -- even when we jump out of airplanes and helicopters. I know that I didn't leave him in the aircraft when I made that last jump; I know he exited the aircraft with me.

And even if I had not survived my 19th jump, I'm convinced that the Lord Jesus would have kept my spirit safe in his care, for in the Bible he says, "I am the resurrection and the life. Anyone who believes in me will live, even after dying."[1] And I believe every word that the Lord Jesus Christ spoke. He can give those who believe in him eternal life because he conquered death itself after his own death on a cross. In fact, that's what Easter is all about – Jesus' victory over death.

---

[1] John 11:25, NLT.

One More Jump?

Later that same day, someone told me that I could still make another jump. I had hoped to jump twice that day so that I could reach my personal goal of 20 jumps, but I decided to stop with 19 jumps and a prayer.

Gene Richardson's Good-Bye Note

Figure 167 Sgt. Gene Richardson wrote a moving good-bye note to his fellow paratroopers after learning that the unit would soon become Armored Cavalry. He found a National Guard Airborne Ranger unit to join in Austin and transfered to it (Photo by author).

As our unit changed from an Airborne unit to an Armored Cavalry unit, I chose not to re-enlist. My good friend Gene Richardson chose to leave our unit for another Airborne unit in the Austin area. When we parted ways for the last time, Gene handed me and some of the other guys who remained in the unit the following note:

_____, (name of recipient), I'm sorry I didn't say good-bye to you. I just couldn't; I'm too emotional. That last day with you was one of the saddest of my life. Never again will we run and march together; never again will we laugh and sing; never again will we endure the heat, the cold, the exhaustion and the hunger; never again will we tell our war stories about tree landings, exits, PLFs; never again will we share our C-Rations, our water, our happiness, our fears.

But I will never forget you, and one of these days, when you are clanking down some road in Eastern Europe, and come across a burned-out old Sergeant, give me a ride.

And when the sun is getting low in your day, and you must go to meet the great Jump Master in the sky, you may hear those around you mutter, "He was a pretty good ole boy, but he didn't amount to much" – well, we know better, and with the last of your strength, raise your fist and give a loud and thunderous "AIRBORNE!"

--Geno,
Sergeant Richardson

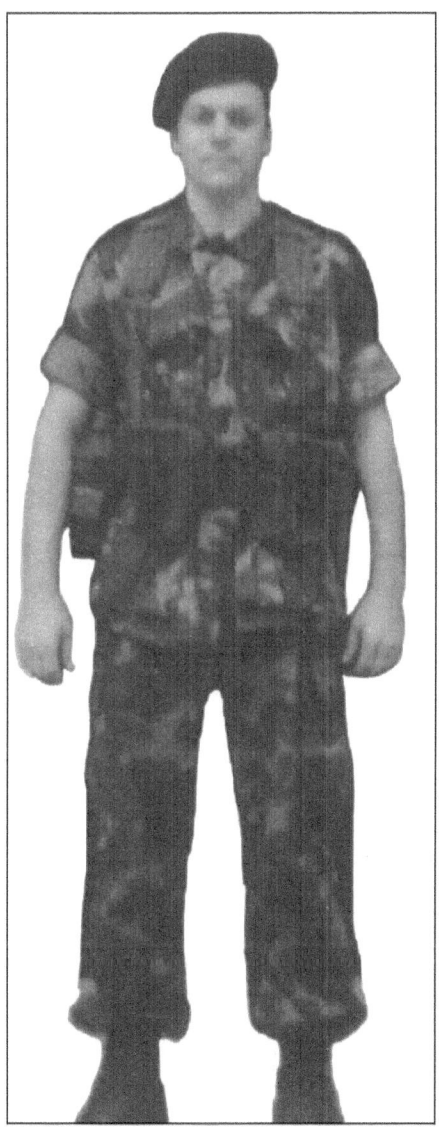

Figure 168 Sgt. Travis Monday while with the 143d Airborne Infantry, 36th Airborne Brigade, Texas Army National Guard (Author's collection).

My Jumping Jack Family

Figure 169 Left to right: Travis, Pam, Tim, and Jared Monday in San Angelo, Texas (Photo by author; December 25, 2005).

Many factors played a part in my decision to write this book at this time in my life, but the Lord motivated me to write it now primarily through my family.

Aviation Orientation of Our Family

Pam, Tim, Jared, and I have all had significant contact with the world of aviation. My father-in-law, William ("Bill") Krebs, flew C-46 and C-47

Army transports in the Pacific during World War II. After the war he piloted civilian airliners until his retirement from Western Airlines. In retirement he purchased a small private airplane, and we all flew in it with him in the skies above Monument, Colorado.

Figure 170 Pam Monday's father, Bill Krebs, flew Army transport airplanes in World War II. Here he is shown in New Guinea with some of the natives (Photo courtesy of Bill Krebs).

Thanks to Bill Krebs, my son Jared also flew in a glider.

Figure 171 Jared Monday (left) with his grandfather, Bill Krebs (center) after flying in a glider (Author's collection).

When Bill Krebs, on February 5, 1982, piloted his final flight for Western Airlines, Pam and I, along with other members of his family, made the trip with him in a DC-10 from San Francisco, California, to Honolulu, Hawaii. I visited him in the cockpit during the flight, and Pam rode in the cockpit with him as he landed in Honolulu. In my journal for that day I included the following comments: "Many congratulations came as Dad ended his thirty-one year career. We arrived exhausted but excited, little Tim having slept most of the flight – a flight he'll not even remember." Tim would not remember the flight or the trip because he was only 1 ½ months old.

Figure 172 Bill Krebs, on the day of his last flight for Western Airlines, holding his grandson, Tim Monday (Author's collection; February 5, 1982).

Later, while Tim attended high school in Sweetwater, Texas, he had an aviation-related experience that he definitely does remember. He and several other students from Sweetwater High School participated in NASA's Texas Fly High Program. This adventure included the experience of weightlessness while flying in a jet aircraft sometimes called "The Vomit Comet." Tim and his friends conducted a scientific experiment in the environment of weightlessness, and they later spoke to the Sweetwater Rotary Club about that experience. At the time I served as treasurer of the Rotary Club and enjoyed hearing him speak to my fellow club members.

Figure 173 Tim Monday (2nd from right) with three other Sweetwater High School students who participated in NASA's Texas Fly High Program. This photo was taken right after the group spoke to the Sweetwater Rotary Club in Sweetwater, Texas (Photo by author; May 9, 2000).

Pam, Tim, and Jared Decide to Jump Out of an Airplane

Pam surprised me one day with the announcement that she wanted to make a parachute jump, and she began making the necessary arrangements.

Since my writing instructors, Stephen and Janet Bly, wanted me to conduct an interview as one of my writing assignments, I asked Pam if I could interview her about her upcoming adventure. She readily agreed. Following is an excerpt from that interview:

Travis: Please explain to me what you plan to do.

Pam: I plan to go skydiving. I'm going to go down with another person. It's called "tandem." We'll jump from an altitude of 10,500 feet.

Travis: Tell me, why would you want to jump out of a perfectly good airplane?

Pam: I just think it would be an experience you'd never forget – a real exciting and thrilling experience. It's something I've always wanted to do and I decided, why not do it?

I guess the thing that really got me set on it is because I wanted to do something really special for 50th birthday. I didn't want my 50th birthday to be something I dreaded; I wanted it to be something I celebrated. I wanted something really special to do to celebrate that occasion, so I picked this.

When Pam told our sons, Tim and Jared, about her plans to go skydiving, they both decided to jump with her. I didn't interview them so you'll have to ask them why they did it.

Skydiving Adventure in Stanton, Texas

Figure 174 Jared Monday glides to earth under a parachute designed like a Texas flag (Photo by author; June 25, 2005).

Pam, Jared, and I on June 25, 2005, traveled to Stanton, Texas, for an adventure in skydiving. In Stanton Tim and his wife Le'Ann joined us at the airport. Since I had already jumped 19 times, I decided not to jump. Instead, I captured the adventure on videotape and in still photos.

After some on-the-spot training, Jared made the first jump. Pam, Tim, and Jared had all decided to jump tandem, that is, they would jump while attached to a more experienced jumper. Jared had a real good experience and walked away from the landing with a huge smile on his face.

Tim jumped next. He, like Jared, had a good experience but he had a rather rough landing, ending up on top of the instructor when they fell backwards after reaching the ground.

Figure 175 Tim Monday prepares to land at the airport in Stanton, Texas (Photo by author; June 25, 2005).

Pam jumped after Tim, but she didn't enjoy her experience as much as Tim and Jared because she got too hot and had some problems with nausea. In spite of those problems, she did what she said she would do;

she jumped out of an airplane in flight and rode a parachute back down to the surface of Planet Earth.

For many years people called me crazy for jumping out of perfectly good airplanes. Now I know that God loves people crazy enough to jump out of a fully functioning aircraft, and that includes my family!

Figure 176 Pam Monday prepares to make a parachute jump (Photo by author; June 25, 2005)

Figure 177 Pam Monday in the sky over Stanton, Texas (Photo by author; June 25, 2005).

Figure 178 Left to right: Tim Monday, Le'Ann (Tim's wife), and Pam Monday on the day of the family parachute jumps (Photo by author; June 25, 2005).

Figure 179 Le'Ann Monday (left) with Pam Monday on the day of the family jumping adventure (June 25, 2005).

Figure 180 Jared Monday right after his skydiving adventure (Photo by author; June 25, 2005).

Figure 181 Tim Monday immediately following his jump (Photo by author; June 25, 2005).

Bibliography

Books

Airborne: 4th Student Battalion (Class Book). Fort Benning, Georgia: Winter, 1971.

Burkett, B. G. and Whitley, Glenna. *Stolen Valor: How the Vietnam Generation Was Robbed of Its Heroes and Its History*. Dallas, Texas: Verity Press, Inc., 1998.

Clancy, Tom. *Airborne: A Guided Tour of an Airborne Task Force*. New York: Berkley Books, 1997.

Cragg, SGM Dan. *Guide to Military Installations: 2nd Edition*. Harrisburg, Pennsylvania: Stackpole Books, 1988.

Dean, Chuck. *Nam Vet: Making Peace with Your Past*. United States of America: WordSmith Publishing, 2000.

Dean, Jimmy and Donna Meade. *Thirty Years of Sausage, Fifty Years of Ham: Jimmy Dean's Own Story*. New York: Berkley Books, 2004.

Delvin, Gerard M. *Paratroopers!* New York: St. Martin's Press, 1979.

Flanagan, E. M., Jr. *Airborne: A Combat History of American Airborne Forces*. New York: Presidio Press Book published by Ballentine Publishing Group, 2002.

Gutzman, Philip. *Vietnam: A Visual Encyclopedia*. London, England: PRC Publishing Ltd., 2002.

Karnow, Stanley. *Vietnam: A History*. New York: The Viking Press, 1983.

Kelley, Michael P. *Where We Were in Vietnam*. Central Point, Oregon:

Hellgate Press, 2002.

Kelly, Daniel E. *Seawolves: First Choice.* New York: Ivy Books, 1998.

Langley, Wanda. *Flying Higher: The Women Airforce Service Pilots of World War II.* North Haven, Connecticut: Linnet Books, 2002.

Lanning, Michael Lee and Cragg, Dan. *Inside the VC and the NVA.* New York: Ballantine Books, 1992.

Mair, George. *A Life with Purpose.* New York: Berkley Books, 2005.

McAlister, George A. *Alamo: The Price of Freedom.* San Antonio, Texas: Docutex, Inc., 1988.

Monday, Travis. *Ultimate Museum Musings.* United States of America: Travis Monday, 2007.

_____. *W. F. Matthews: Lost Battalion Survivor.* United States of America: Lulu Enterprises, Inc., 2004.

_____. *Wings, WASP, & Warriors.* United States of America: Lulu Enterprises, Inc., 2005.

Monde, Bennet B. *Wings Over Sweetwater: The History of Avenger Field.* Bennet B. Monde, 1995.

Spector, Ronald H. *After Tet: The Bloodiest Year in Vietnam.* New York: The Free Press, 1993.

Stanton, Shelby L. *The Rise and Fall of an American Army.* Novato, California: Presidio Press, 1985.

_____. *Vietnam Order of Battle.* New York: Galahad Books, 1986.

Technical Training of Parachutists: TM 57-220. Washington, D. C.: Department of the Army Headquarters, June 1968.

Thompson, Leroy. *The All Americans: The 82nd Airborne.* Great Britain: David & Charles Publishers, 1988.

Thompson, W. Oscar. *Concentric Circles of Concern.* Nashville, Tennessee: Broadman Press, 1981.

Warren, Rick. *The Purpose Driven Life.* Grand Rapids, Michigan: Zondervan, 2002.

Weeks, John. *Assault from the Sky: A History of Airborne Warfare.* New York: G. P. Putnam's Sons, 1978.

Yeats, E. L., and Shelton, Hooper. *History of Nolan County, Texas.* Sweetwater, Texas: Shelton Press, 1975.

Newspapers

Abilene Reporter-News, 20 February 2005.

Abilene Reporter-News, 28 July 2004.

Parrott, Joshua. "From Military to Ministry." *San Angelo Standard-Times*, 5 July 2003.

Plainview Daily Herald, 8 March 2005.

Plainview Daily Herald, 9 December 2005.

San Angelo Standard-Times, 22 June 2002.

San Angelo Standard-Times, 27 July 2002.

San Angelo Standard-Times, 24 August 2002.

San Angelo Standard-Times, 12 June 2004.

Sweetwater Reporter, 19 July 2002.

Sweetwater Reporter, 2 December 2005.

Correspondence and Interviews

Herschel Carmichael, San Angelo, Texas. Interview with Author, 28 February 2006.

Lillian (Pratt) Carter, Eula, Texas. Interview with Author, 23 September 2005.

_____. Eula, Texas. Interview with Author, 3 November 2005.

William Otto Carter, Jr., Eula, Texas. Interview with William Otto Carter, III, n.d.

William Otto Carter, III, Eula, Texas. Interview by Author, 23 September 2005.

Robert E. Dils, San Angelo, Texas. Interview by Author, 8 September 2005.

Rigdon Edwards, Sweetwater, Texas. Interview with Author, 4 June 1997.

Ronald Roy Hansen, San Angelo, Texas. Interview with Author, 6 October 2005.

Gerald T. Luchino. Letter to Author, 29 November 1990.

W. F. Matthews, San Angelo, Texas. Interview with Author, 26 September 2002.

W. F. Matthews, San Angelo, Texas. Interview with Author, 21 November 2003.

Joe Monday, Portales, New Mexico. Interview with Author, 18 November 1997.

Pamela Jean Monday, San Angelo, Texas. Interview with Author, 21 May 2005.

Bennet B. Monde, Sweetwater, Texas. Interview with Author, 29 May 1997.

John S. Nichols. Letter to Author, 22 July 2003.

Lorraine Zillner Rodgers, Sweetwater, Texas. Interview with Author, 5 October 2000.

H. B. Stevens, Sweetwater, Texas. Interview with Author, 25 September 2000.

Armando Vasquez, San Angelo, Texas. Interview with Author, 10 November 2005.

Other Sources

Army Chaplain Corps: A Brief History (U.S. Army Chaplain Museum Fort Jackson, South Carolina. From website (June 12 2005).

Beben, Lt. Joe. "Big Tet -- 1968." Posted by Robert Crowley. http://www.military.com/HomePage/UnitPageHistory/1,13506 771026,00. Html 8/20/2005.

Carter, William Otto, Jr., "Autobiography of William Otto Carter, Jr." An unpublished and undated article provided by the Carter family.

Handbook of Texas Online.

Index

101ˢᵗ Airborne Division, 141, 143, 144, 145, 147, 159, 160, 167, 193

101ˢᵗ Airborne Division (Airmobile), 143, 159, 169, 170

101ˢᵗ Airborne Division arrived in Vietnam, 144

101ˢᵗ Airborne Division had shifted, 144

101ˢᵗ Airborne Division left its home, 160

101st Airborne Division Screaming Eagles, 143

101ˢᵗ Division, 145

105 mm artillery round exploded, 147

105s, 119, 120

143d Airborne Infantry, 195, 196, 204, 249, 250, 255

143d Airborne Infantry (photo), 202, 206, 208

143d Airborne Infantry in Arlington, Texas, 249

143d Airborne Infantry Regiment, 192

143d Airborne Infantry Regiment, 36ᵗʰ Airborne Brigade, 192

143d Airborne Infantry waiting to board (photo), 207

143d Airborne Infantry, 36th Airborne Brigade, Texas Army National Guard, 255

143d Airborne returning from a patrol (photo), 202

173ᵈ Airborne Brigade, 159, 167, 168, 169

173d Airborne Brigade shoulder patch (photo), 168

173ᵈ Airborne Brigade Sky Soldiers, 167

173ᵈ Airborne Engineer Company, 169

173ᵈ became the first, 168

173ᵈ Infantry Brigade in 1917, 167

173d paid an enormous price, 168

173ᵈ was deactivated on, 169

Index

19 jumps and a prayer, 253

1967 Hill Fights, 240

1968, Viet Cong forces assaulted, 114

19th jump, I came face-to-face with death, 251

20th Engineer Brigade, 112, 113, 114

20th Engineer Brigade deployed to Vietnam, 112

20th Engineer Brigade patch, 112

250 Foot Free Towers, 81, 87

250 Foot Tower, 87

250 Foot Towers, 79, 87

250 Foot Towers at Fort Benning (photo), 79, 80

250 Foot Towers at Fort Benning, Georgia, 79

250 Foot Towers in use at Fort Benning (photo), 88

26th Tennessee Infantry, 160, 161

2nd Battalion, 131st Field Artillery, 192

3.5 Rocket Launcher, 46

326th Airborne Engineer Battalion, 145

326th Engineer Battalion, 145, 146, 147, 150, 154, 159, 160, 169

326th Engineer Battalion (Airmobile), 145

326th Engineer Battalion (photo), 147, 156

326th Engineer Battalion at Fort Jackson, South Carolina, 145

326th Engineer Battalion, 101st Airborne Division (Airmobile), 159

326th Engineer Battalion, 101st Airborne Division(photo), 147

326th Engineers (Combat), 145

326th Engineers began on, 145

326th was deactivated, 145

34 Foot Mock Tower, 74

34 Foot Mock Tower at Fort Benning (photo), 78

34 Foot Mock Towers at Fort Benning (photo), 75

34 Foot Tower, 87

34th Engineer Group, 112, 114, 133

34th Engineer Group sign that says, "Re-Up!", 134

36th Airborne Brigade, 192, 255

36th Airborne Brigade, Texas Army National Guard, 255

36th Infantry Division, 192, 193

43rd and 47th Companies of the 4th Student Battalion, 69

47th Company, 69, 97

520th and 537th Personnel Service Companies, 239

537th Personnel Service Company, 239

62B10 – Heavy Equipment Repairman, 58

69th Engineer Battalion, 111, 112, 114, 126, 127, 137, 141, 237

69th Engineer Battalion (photo), 128, 129

69th Engineer Battalion at Can Tho, 114

69th Engineer Battalion ended up in the thick of battle, 114

69th Engineer Battalion in Vietnam, 137

69th Engineer Battalion in Vietnam (photo), 109

69th Engineer Battalion left Fort Hood, Texas, 114

69th Engineer Battalion would soon return, 141

69th Engineers, 127

75th Airborne Rangers in Vietnam, 232

82nd Airborne, 194

82nd Airborne Division, 91, 92, 194

87th Division, 167

87th Reconnaissance Troop of the 87th Division, 167

90th Replacement Battalion, 110

9th Infantry, 134

A Life with Purpose (book), 201

A.S.N. Night Fighters Squadron, 19

A-3-4, Class 10, 60

A-4 Skyhawk, 18

Abdullah, CPL, 114

Abilene (Texas) as a surgical orderly, 188

Abilene (Texas) I served as Minister of Youth, 187

Abilene Writers Guild, 184

Abilene, Texas, 90, 103, 105, 177, 180, 181, 182, 183, 184, 187, 188, 189, 218, 223, 231

Abilene's (Texas) friendly atmosphere, 180

Absent Without Leave (AWOL), 40

AC-119 gun ships, 90

Adopt-an-Orphan Day, 154

Advanced Individual Training (AIT), 52, 53, 58, 59, 69, 70, 238, 239

Agnew, Vice-President Spiro T., 170

Air Cavalry Stetson (photo), 108

Air Corps, 19

Airborne, 13, 65, 71, 72, 97, 205, 253

Index

Airborne again!, 192

Airborne Chapel at Fort Benning, 85

Airborne Chapel at Fort Benning (photo), 85

Airborne Chaplain at Fort Benning, 85

Airborne Class Book, 76, 85

Airborne Course, 71, 73

Airborne discipline and expectations, 72

Airborne history, 81

Airborne Infantry, 201, 250, 251

Airborne Infantry unit of the Texas, 188

Airborne P.T. (physical training), 72

Airborne Physical Training Test, 62

Airborne Ranger, 41, 198

Airborne Rangers, 193

Airborne School, 1, 27, 46, 57, 58, 62, 67, 69, 81, 82, 85, 86, 89, 90, 92, 97, 99, 252

Airborne School Class Book, 71

Airborne School diploma (image), 98

Airborne Shuffle, 8, 84

Airborne students gain control of their parachutes (photo), 95

Airborne students inside of an airplane (photo), 6

Airborne Test Platoon, 80

Airborne to Chairborne, 177

Airborne training, 1

Airborne unit in Arlington, Texas, 191

Airborne!, 144

AIRBORNE!, 254

Airborne: A Guided Tour of an Airborne Task Force (book), 67

Airbubble!, 144

Airmobile, 143, 144, 159, 169

Airmobile!, 144

Alabama, 10, 95, 236

Alamo, 24, 25, 122, 187

Alamo addiction, 25

Alamo commander William Barrett Travis, 24

Alamo crazy, 25

Alamo defenders, 122

Alamo for my school project, 24

Alaska, 107

Alberto Rodriguez Hall in San Angelo, Texas (photo), 234

Alexander, Evelyn, 213

Alexander, Hall, 213

Alexander, Jeff, 213

Alexander, Natalie, 213

Alexanders (Hall, Evelyn, Jeff, and Natalie), 213

All Americans, 91, 194

All Americans of the 82nd Airborne Division, 194

ALL THE WAY one more time, 192

All the Way!, 72

Allen, James, 24

All-Vets Council, 241

All-Vets Council of San Angelo resurrected, 241

All-Vets Council, played a significant role, 241

Amarillo, Texas, 27, 35, 36, 99, 103

America, 14, 23, 99, 145, 221, 226

America – love it or leave it!, 99

America one nation, under God, 221

America's Army Special Forces, 25

America's Bicentennial Year, 182

America's involvement in Vietnam, 183

American Airborne, 68

American Airborne history, 81

American Civil War, 113

American heroes, 114

American ideals of patriotism, 25

American influence is everywhere, 120

American paratroopers surrender or, 144

American patriot, 25

American Revolution, 162

American soldiers were knifed, 139

Americans, 26, 35, 99, 102, 119, 153, 168

Americans back the World, 119

Americans who served in Vietnam, 102

Among the Dead (poem), 117

Amy, Michael, 117

Anchorage, Alaska, 107

Anderson Hall (HSU), 181

Angelo State University (ASU), 231, 238

Anson, Texas, 187

Antelope (drop zone), 203

Index

Application for Airborne Training, 62

apprentice pastor to Rev. Roy Belcher, 187

AR 611-7, 62

Arkansas, 194, 195, 196, 202, 209

Arkansas (photo), 209

Arlington, Texas, 79, 188, 191, 192, 193, 194, 201, 249

Armed Forces Day, 237

Armored Cavalry, 205, 250, 251, 253

Armored Cavalry operations, 251

Armored Cavalry training, 251

Arms Secure Peace (motto), 193

Army Airborne Infantry, 193

Army Airborne Rangers, 193

Army bulldozer (photo), 59

Army chaplain, 191

Army chaplain at Fort Benning, 252

Army Engineer cadence song, 57

Army Engineers, 58, 193

Army Engineers have a proud tradition of service, 58

Army in Korea, 20

Army in the Pacific, 19

Army Infantry, 193

Army National Guard, 60, 61

Army of the Republic of South Vietnam (ARVN), 115, 134

Army on Guadalcanal, 20

Army Reserves, 61

Army Special Forces, 25

Army trainees arriving at Fort Ord (photo), 37

Army, Institute of Heraldry, 113

Army's Engineer Equipment Repairman Course, 65

Arnold, Edward, 54

Arnold, Edward (photo), 53

Arrowhead DZ, 196

ARVN Rangers made contact, 124

Austin Peay State University, 161, 177

Austin Peay State University in Clarksville, Tennessee, 177

Austin, Texas, 22, 251, 253

Australians, 134

author in a rubber raft (photo), 209

author receiving his Master of Divinity degree (photo), 211

author with a fellow soldier in the woods (photo), 175

author with his future wife, Pamela Jean Krebs (photo), 181

author's discharge from the Texas Army National Guard (image), 251

author's grandfather (right), on a horse (photo), 29

author's high school diploma (image), 28

author's ministry card as an Outpost Director (image), 218

author's uncle L. J. Williams (photo), 32

Auto Mechanics, 21

Auto Mechanics at Plainview High School, 58

Auto Mechanics Chapter 328, 22

Auto Mechanics Class, 22, 62

Auto Mechanics program, 27

Autry, Gene, 167

Avenger Field (Sweetwater, TX), 86, 224, 225

Awalt, Jimmy, 26, 179, 231

Awalt, Roger, 26, 179

AWOL (absent without leave), 162

Bachelor of Arts degree in Bible and English, 187

Bachelor of Science degree in Physical Recreation, 188

Back in the Saddle Again (song), 167

Ballad of the Basic Combat Trainee (poem), 37

Ballad of the Green Berets (song), 25

Baptist Student Union, 186

Barnes, Lt. Governor Ben, 22

barracks at Fort Campbell (photo), 174

barracks at Fort Ord, California (photo), 40

barracks building at Fort Ord (photo), 49

Barton, Barbara, 227

Basic Airborne Course (BAC), 71

Basic Combat Training at Fort Bliss, Texas, 239

Basic Combat Training at Fort Polk, Louisiana, 238

Basic Training (Army), 5, 11, 26, 37, 38, 39, 40, 41, 46, 47, 49, 58, 64, 117, 237, 239

Basic Training (Army) (photo), 42, 49

Basic Training(Army), 44

Bastogne, 144, 145

Index

Battle of Fort Donelson, 160, 161

Battle of Freedom Hill, 23

Battle of Nashville, 161

Batty, Betty, 25

Bazooka, 46

Bear Cat (aka Long Thanh), 101

Belcher (Rev. Roy) at Mercer Island Baptist Church, 187

Belcher (Rev. Roy) tied the knot for us, 182

Belcher, (Rev. Roy) pastor of Mercer Island Baptist Church, 182

Belcher, Rev. Roy, 182, 187

Benning, (Henry L.) a soldier from Columbus, 68

Benning, Confederate Gen. Henry L., 68

Bergin, Robert, 181

best friend (James Robb) at Fort Leonard Wood, 53

best friend at Hardin-Simmons University, John Mitton (photo), 180

best friend in the 69th Engineers, Bob Dils, 127

best friend up north was John G. Owens, 150

best friend, John Mitton, 181

best person (Pam) that ever happened to me, 182

Bethel Baptist Church (Plainview, TX), 178

Bethel Baptist Church (Plainview, TX) (photo), 178

Bible, 105, 164, 165, 172, 173, 187, 252

Bible studies, 165

Bien Hoa, South Vietnam, 102, 109, 110, 239

Big John (song), 17

Big Spring, Texas, 232, 245

Binh Thuy Naval Base, 111, 127

Binh Thuy North, South Vietnam, 139

Binh Thuy North, South Vietnam (photo), 142

Binh Thuy, South Vietnam, 111, 114, 115, 122, 127, 135, 137, 143

Black Beret of the Army Airborne Rangers, 193

Black Hats, 71, 72, 73, 74, 76, 81, 95, 203

Black Hats are the tribal elders, 72

Black Hats taught me never to anticipate, 203

Black Ponies out of Binh Thuy, 122

Blair, Ronnie, 218

Blood on the Risers (song), 2, 84

Blue Pups (football team), 20

Bly (Stephen & Janet), wanted me to conduct, 260

Bly, Janet, 260

Bly, Stephen, 260

boarding a C-119 Flying Boxcar (photo), 94

Bob Hope Christmas Special, 152, 153

Bond, Kenneth, 105

book called, *Concentric Circles of Concern*, 201

book *Wings Over Sweetwater*, 224

book, *Airborne: A Guided Tour of an Airborne Task Force*, 67

book, *Inside the VC and the NVA*, 126

book, *Nineteen Jumps and a Prayer*, 250

book, *Seawolves: First Choice*, 134

book, *The Purpose Driven Life*, 200

Boone, Daniel, 186

Boone's (Daniel) grave, 186

Box (Eldon) from Plainview survived, 133

Box (Eldon) of Plainview served as a, 26

Box (Eldon) play his guitar, 150

Box, Eldon, 26, 133, 150

Bridges (Becky) worked with me as art editor, 185

Bridges, (Dr. Julian) taught sociology at Hardin-Simmons, 185

Bridges, Becky, 181, 185

Bridges, Dr. Julian, 185

Briggs at Tan Hoa (photo), 109

Briggs, Lester, 127

Briggs, Lester (photo), 109, 130

Bright (Tom) attended a ceremony, 232

Bright (Tom) joined with Armando Vasquez to help, 233

Bright (Tom), and some other, 233

Bright, Tom, 232, 233

Bright, Tom (photo), 233

British, 162

Bronze Star, 154

Brown, Trent (photo), 105

Bryan Baptist Association, Okalhoma, 213

BT-13, 225

bucket loader (photo), 63

Buddy Plan, 26, 39, 69

Builders for Peace (motto), 114

Building Combat Power (motto), 113

bunker in which the author (photo), 149

Bush (Governor) arrived in Abilene, 223

Bush (Governor) is about to speak, 223

Bush (President George H. W.) had made an emergency, 223

Bush (President George H. W.) later made two more, 223

Bush (President George H. W.) made several parachute jumps, 223

Bush, Governor, 223

Bush, President George H. W., 223

Bush, President George H. W. (photo), 223

Butch Cassidy and the Sundance Kid (movie), 106

C Company, 326th Engineer Battalion, 169, 171, 173

C-119 Flying Boxcar, 2, 4, 7, 9, 10, 89, 90, 94, 97

C-119 Flying Boxcar (photo), 2, 4, 94

C-119s during the Korean War, 89

C-130 drops paratroopers (photo), 206

C-130 Hercules, 73, 76, 84, 89, 90, 97, 143, 169, 172, 200, 203

C-130 Hercules (photo), 90, 206

C-130 Mock Exit Assembly, 73, 74

C-130's then flew us back to Dallas, 200

C-141 for a jump (photo), 207

C-141 Starlifter, 90, 197, 204, 208

C-141 Starlifter (photo), 191, 197, 207, 208

C-141 Starlifter drops paratroopers (photo), 208

C-46, 257

C-46 and C-47 Army transports, 258

C-47, 257

California, 5, 35, 36, 37, 40, 43, 48, 49, 51, 64, 106, 200, 259

California, 39

California's early history, 36

Calvary Baptist Church (Colorado City, TX), 186, 215, 216, 222

Camp Alpha in Saigon, 111

Camp Campbell, 159

Camp Cummings near Knoxville, Tennessee, 161

Camp Cummings, Tennessee, 161

Camp Dix, New Jersey, 167

Camp Eagle, 146, 152, 153

Camp Wilkinson, 146, 147, 148, 151, 152, 154

Camp Wilkinson (photo), 156

Camp Wilkinson had been built, 146

Camp Wilkinson near Phu Bai (photo), 147

Camp Wilkinson(photo), 147

Camp Wilkinson, I could no longer, 147

Camp Wilkinson, I did not sleep much, 148

Camp Wilkinson, located two km southeast, 146

Campbell (Fort) was named after Brigadier General, 159

Campbell, (Gen. William Bowen) a former governor, 159

Campbell, Gen. William Bowen, 159

Can Tho Army Airfield, 114

Can Tho, South Vietnam, 114, 115, 164

Can Tho, South Vietnam (photo), 113

canopy, 9, 95

Canyon, Texas, 103

Carmichael (Herschel) at the Concho Valley Vietnam Veterans Memorial (photo), 236

Carmichael (Herschel) told me how, 236

Carmichael (Herschel) went through Basic Combat Training, 239

Carmichael (Herschel), at that time served as president, 239

Carmichael (Robert), a veteran of the, 238

Carmichael, Herschel, 233, 236, 239

Carmichael, Robert, 238

Carroll (Gov. Julian M.) declaring us honorary Kentucky Colonels, 186

Carroll, Governor Julian M., 186

Carter (Otto, Jr.) standing beside a P-47, 230

Carter, Jr., (Otto) with one of his two P-47 (photo), 230

Carter, Lillian, 231

Carter, Otto, III, 231

Carter, Otto, Jr., 230, 231

Carter, Otto, Jr. (photo), 230

Casper, Ken, 227

Catch-22 (book), 104

Catch-22 (movie), 104

Index 283

Catch-22 contributed to that inner conflict, 105

Catholic priest arranged for us to, 154

Catholic priest remained in-country, 154

Central Chapel (Fort Campbell, KY), 173

CH-47 Chinook, 196, 198, 199, 204, 250

CH-47 Chinook (photo), 195

Chapel at Fort Benning (photo), 85

chaplain, 85, 187, 191, 201, 240

chaplain at Fort Benning, 252

chaplain in the State of Wisconsin, 240

chaplain of the Vietnam Veterans of America, Chapter 457, 239

chaplain of VVA 457, 240

Charlie Cong, 41

check equipment, 7

Christian, 172

Christian environment and the academic setting, 180

Christians, 166

Christmas, 221

Christmas Eve, 153

Christmas Eve, 1971, 152

Christmas morning, 154

Christmas morning, 1971, 154

Christmas morning, Hawkins and I waited, 154

Christmas Special, 152

Christmas Special to the 101st Airborne Division, 152

Churchhill Downs, 186

City Hall (Sweetwater, TX), 226

Civil War, 113, 160

Civil War installation near Clarksville, 160

Clancy (Tom) calls his section, 67

Clancy (Tom) explains, "Nobody in the U. S. Army", 69

Clancy (Tom) indicates that the survivors, 77

Clancy (Tom) says of these instructors, 72

Clancy, Tom, 67, 69, 77

Clarksville, Tennessee, 159, 160, 161, 177

Class 24, 69

Class of 1970, 26

Clayton (Dr. Lawrence) walking toward me, 186

Clayton, (Dr. Lawrence) an English professor at Hardin-Simmons, 185

Clayton, (Dr. Lawrence) and he always urged me, 185

Clayton, Dr. Lawrence, 185, 186

Clayton's (Dr. Lawrence) influence, I edited, 185

Clifford (Hanley W.) served as our executive officer, 69

Clifford, Lt. Hanley W., 69

Co. A, 3rd Bn., AIT Bde, 59

Cobra gun ships, 122

Cobras, 122

Coleman, PFC, 114

collapse of South Vietnam, 183

college magazine, *The Corral*, 185

Colonel Travis, 187

Colonel's House, 186

Colorado, 258

Colorado City, Texas, 80, 186, 215, 216, 219, 220, 222, 245, 246

Colorado City, Texas (photo), 219

Colorado Middle School (Colorado City, TX), 220

Columbus, Georgia, 68

Combat Equipment Jump, 95

Company A, 3rd Battalion, 4th AIT Brigade, USATC Engineers, 59

Company B, 1st Battalion (Airborne), 143d Infantry, 193

Company C (326th Engr Bn) was jumping, 169

Company C, 326th Engineer Battalion, 169

Company C, 326th Engineer Battalion, 101st Airborne Division (Airmobile), 169

Company H, Battalion 2, Brigade 1, 38

Concentric Circles of Concern (book), 201

Concho Valley Vietnam Veterans, 233

Concho Valley Vietnam Veterans Memorial (photo), 248

Concho Valley Vietnam Veterans Memorial (San Angelo, TX), 235, 236, 237

Concho Valley Vietnam Veterans Memorial at Mathis Field (photo), 236

Concho Valley Vietnam Veterans of America, Chapter 457, 231

Concho Valley Vietnam Veterans), 233

Confederacy, 160

Index

Confederate Army, 161

Confederate re-enactors (photo), 161

Confederates, 161

Cook, Gary, 25

Cook, Mark, 180

Coronado Junior High, 20

Coronado Junior High School, 100

COSVN Resolution Number 9, 126

Cradle of American Airborne, 68

Cragg, Dan, 126

Crockett, Davy, 25

Crowder, (Dickie) spent most of my, 100

Crowder, Dickie ("Duke"), 100, 151

Cumberland County, Tennessee, 162

Cupp (Franzas) had set up a WASP Room, 224

Cupp, Museum Director Franzas, 224

Currie (Private) a lift at the Leadership Academy (photo), 55

cut hair in her home, 17

cutting hair in Plainview, 29

Cyrus, (Billy Ray) that "all gave some – some gave all", 221

Cyrus, Billy Ray, 221

D Company (69th Engr Bn) moved three times during, 139

D Company of the 69th Engineer Battalion (photo), 129

D Company, 69th Engineer Battalion, 115, 117, 120, 121, 137, 139, 237

D Company, 69th Engineer Battalion (photo), 128

D.I.s (Drill Instructors) of Jump School, 71

D.I.s pushed us hard, 44

D.I.s reprimanded us for, 43

DA FORM 2496, 62

Da Nang to deliver the equipment, 152

Da Nang, South Vietnam, 143, 152, 155

Dallas at Redbird Drop Zone, 204

Dallas, Texas, 193, 198, 199, 200, 204, 250

Darby, Dr. Pres, 227

Dash-1, a modified T-10, 204

Davidson, Major Gen. Phillip B, Jr., 35

Davis (Tom) developed a symbol, 243

Davis (Tom) developed a symbol for, 242

Davis, Tom, 233, 243

Davis, Tom (photo), 242

Dayton, Ohio, 237

DC-10, 259

Dean (Chuck) called *Nam Vet: Making Peace with Your Past*, 217

Dean (Jimmy) speaks of his mother cutting hair, 16

Dean (left) and Lee Monday (photo), 146

Dean (Ruth) was cutting my hair, 16

Dean (Ruth), the mother of the famous entertainer, 15

Dean, Chuck, 216, 217

Dean, Don, 16, 17

Dean, Jimmy, 15, 16, 17

Dean, Ruth, 15

Dean's (Chuck) book *Nam Vet*, 218

Delta Developers, 113, 114

Denison, Texas, 215

Denny (Sgt. Billie E.) A former Green Beret, 171

Denny, Sgt. Billie E., 171

Denver (John) wrote the song, 107

Denver, John, 107

Department of the Army, 113

Det 7 (Detachment 7), 137

Detachment 7, 137

DF11, thirty-six men, 19

DF74, lost thirty-four men, 19

Dils (Robert) and I both had at times questioned, 238

Dils (Robert) and me standing in front of, 133

Dils (Robert) is a Vietnam veteran who, 238

Dils (Robert) what stood out in his memory, 238

Dils (Robert) with Travis Monday in San Angelo (photo), 237

Dils (Robert), born on January 4, 237

Dils (Robert), my best friend in Vietnam during, 237

Dils (Robert), the author's best friend (photo), 129

Dils at Binh Thuy North (photo), 142

Dils at Tan Hoa (photo), 130

Dils jokingly point to a sign that (photo), 133

Dils, Robert (Bob), 127, 133, 237, 238

Index

Dils, Robert (Bob) (photo), 129, 130, 133, 142, 237

Dils' (Robert) visit allowed me to interview, 237

Director of Missions of Bryan Baptist Association, 213

Disney watched with envy, 153

Disney, Walt, 25, 153

Distinctive Unit Insignia, 145

Doctor of Ministry degree, 222

dog named J. B. had been with our outfit, 137

Door Gunner School, 132, 134

Door Gunner's School, 133

drawing by the author as a 6-year-old child, 23

Drill Instructors (D.I.s), 38, 39, 40, 42, 43, 44, 45, 71

Drill Sergeants, 38, 39

Drop Zone (DZ), 5, 76, 200

drop zone was called Antelope, 203

Dyess Air Force Base in Abilene, Texas (photo), 90

DZ Fryar, 97

DZ was at Fort Hood, 200

E Company, 26th Tennessee Infantry, 160, 161

Eastern Europe, 254

Eastern Tennessee, 162

Edwards (Jim), a former president of VVA 457, 241

Edwards (Rigdon) helped the author (photo), 224

Edwards, (Jim) told me that he was the current, 231

Edwards, (Rigdon) a former flight, 224

Edwards, Jim, 231, 241

Edwards, Jim (photo), 241

Edwards, Rigdon, 223

Edwards, Rigdon (photo), 224

Ellis, Bob, 181

Ellis, Dr. Ray Ellis, 180

Engineer Equipment Repairman Course, 59, 65

Engineer Equipment Repairman School, 58

England, 65

English, 177, 187

entrance to Camp Wilkinson (photo), 156

equipment check, 7

Equipment Jump, 172

Equipment Jumps, 93

escape from a wind-blown parachute (photo), 83

Estacado Junior High, 20

Estes, Allen, 180

European Theatre, 192

evacuation of a young Vietnamese girl, 123

evacuation of the soldier with malaria (photo), 123

Evans (Sgt. James) as our top NCO, 69

Evans, Sgt. James, 69

F Troop, 1st Squadron, 9th Air Calvary, 101

F-4 Phantom, 18

fall of South Vietnam, 184

fall of the Republic of South Vietnam, 183

Fannin, Colonel, 24

Field Radio School, 51, 52, 59

Field Radio School at Fort Ord, 59

Fire Support Base Mary Ann, 116, 139

First Baptist Church (Abilene, TX), 182

Five Basic Jump Techniques, 76

five points of contact, 73

Flanagan, E. M., Jr., 168

Flanagan, Jr., (E. M.) says, "The 173d paid an enormous", 168

Flowers (Jerry) invited me to join, 235

Flowers (Jerry) invited the author to join, 235

Flowers, Jerry, 235

Flowers, Jerry (photo), 235

Floydada, Texas, 14, 15, 25, 220

Ford (President Gerald) a letter expressing my feelings, 183

Ford, President Gerald, 183

Forshey, Marshall, 97

Fort Benning, Georgia, 1, 2, 64, 68, 69, 70, 79, 80, 81, 85, 90, 91, 99, 252

Fort Benning, Georgia (photo), 68, 70, 75, 78, 79, 80, 81, 83, 85, 88, 91, 93, 94

Fort Bliss, Texas, 239

Fort Bragg, North Carolina, 89, 91, 92, 112, 113

Fort Campbell, Kentucky, 145, 159, 160, 162, 169, 171, 172, 183, 186

Fort Campbell, Kentucky (photo), 165, 166, 174, 175

Fort Chaffee, Arkansas, 194, 195, 196, 197

Fort Chaffee, Arkansas (photo), 202, 209

Fort Concho in San Angelo, Texas (photo), 161

Fort Donelson in Tennessee, 160

Fort Donelson, Tennessee, 160, 161

Fort Hood (Texas) for live-fire, 200

Fort Hood on Rapedo Drop Zone, 204

Fort Hood, Texas, 111, 114, 141, 200, 202, 204

Fort Jackson, South Carolina, 145

Fort Leonard Wood, Missouri, 51, 52, 53, 58, 59, 61, 62, 64, 70, 92, 132, 238, 239

Fort Leonard Wood, Missouri (photo), 55, 60, 63

Fort Leonard, Missouri, 51

Fort Lewis, Washington, 114

Fort Lost in the Woods, Misery, 52

Fort Ord, California, 5, 35, 36, 47, 49, 51, 52, 58, 59, 64, 70

Fort Ord, California (photo), 37, 39, 40, 43, 48, 49

Fort Polk, Louisiana, 238

Fort Rucker, Alabama, 236

Fort Worth, Texas, 188, 195, 198, 200, 211, 212

Fort Worth's Harris Hospital, 212

Forth Worth, Texas, 240

France, 167

Franklin (Benjamin) with inventing the concept, 68

Franklin, Benjamin, 68

free country, 221

freedom, 23, 24, 25, 26, 105, 221, 228, 242

Freedom Bird, 155

freedom of oppressed peoples, 25

freefalling, 6

Fremont's Army, 36

Fudge, Ronnie, 20

fully functioning aircraft, 263

Gafford, Chuck, 181

Gannaway, Emily (drawing by), 246

Garland Street Church of Christ in Plainview, 101

Geiger, T. J., 222

Georgia, 1, 10, 64, 68, 70, 75, 78, 79, 80, 85, 88, 94, 99, 150, 252

Germans, 19, 144

Germans at Bastogne, 144

Germans had them surrounded, 144

Germany, 19, 65, 150

Germany with its army, 19

Geronimo, 9

Gideon Bible, 164

Gillis, (Shannon) my immediate supervisor, 150

Gillis, Sgt. Shannon, 150

Go! (Jump Command), 7, 93

God, 164, 170, 172, 173, 177, 180, 191, 201, 213, 214, 215, 216, 217, 218, 221, 252, 263

God bless America!, 221

God blessed me with many good friends, 180

God had blessed us, 215

God has been faithful, 213

God heard my prayer, 164

God loves people crazy enough to, 263

God might want me to, 191

God so loved the world, 164

God to guide me, 216

God used Dean's (Chuck) book, 217

God using it, 217

God wanted me to spend, 177

God would help me overcome it, 216

God's call to preach the Bible, 105

God's forgiveness, 173

God's help for their PTSD, 217

God's leadership, 218

God's presence, 164

God's truth had set me free, 165

God's will, 191, 194

God-given opportunities, 221

Goliad, 24

Goodfellow Air Force Base, 247

Goodfellow Air Force Base (San Angelo, TX), 231

Gospel Ministry, 178, 213, 214

Gospel of Jesus Christ, 178

Gottshall, Dave, 227

Grant (Ulysses S.) got the name, "No-Surrender Grant", 161

Grant during the Civil War (photo), 160

Index 291

Grant, Gen. Ulysses S., 161

Grant, Gen. Ulysses S. (photo), 160

grave of Steve Seigler (photo), 179

Greek Class of Dr. Ray Ellis, 180

Green (Martin) and I both started AIT, 58

Green (Martin) and Travis Monday at Fort Benning, Georgia (photo), 70

Green (Martin) chose to enlist with me, 26

Green (Martin) had signed up for LPC, 52

Green (Martin) leaves for Fort Bragg, 89

Green (Martin) left Fort Benning for Fort Bragg, 91

Green (Martin) made his first two jumps today, 87

Green (Martin) of Plainview, Texas, at Fort Ord (photo), 39

Green (Martin) remained there for Field Radio School, 51

Green at Fort Benning (photo), 91

Green Beret, 25, 38, 193

Green Beret of the Special Forces, 193

Green Berets, 25, 134

Green, (Martin) went to the 82nd Airborne Division, 92

Green, (Martin) who had joined the Army, 69

Green, Billy C., 20

Green, Martin, 26, 36, 38, 40, 44, 47, 51, 52, 58, 59, 69, 87, 88, 89, 91, 92

Green, Martin (photo), 39, 48, 70, 91

Green, Martin and I graduated from Basic, 47

Green, Martin and I thrived in the context of, 40

Green, Martin and I, along with two other Texans, 36

Green, Martin and me assigned to the, 38

Green, Martin completed Jump School, 88

Green, Martin joined the Army with the author, 39

Green, Martin, shared my enthusiasm and also excelled, 38

Greer, (Doug) who served in Vietnam, 218

Greer, Doug, 218

Greer, Doug (photo), 219

Ground Week, 71, 73, 74, 77

guard duty among the dead, 117

guard tower in the motor pool -- a graveyard, 117

guard tower in the motor pool (photo), 118

gung ho, 38

H-2-1, 38

Hansen (Roy) accepted Jesus Christ, 240

Hansen (Roy) has since made 3 missionary, 240

Hansen (Roy) served as chaplain of the Vietnam Veterans of America (photo), 239

Hansen (Roy) served in Vietnam, 240

Hansen (Roy) spent a good number, 240

Hansen (Roy) was a Vietnam veteran who, 240

Hansen (Roy), I made friends with him, 240

Hansen, Roy, 240

Hansen, Roy (photo), 239

Hansen, Roy stepped down as chaplain, 240

Hardin-Simmons could get rough, 180

Hardin-Simmons University, 177, 180, 181, 183, 184, 186

Hardin-Simmons University (HSU), 180, 187, 188, 189

Hardin-Simmons University (HSU) (photo), 190

Hardin-Simmons University in Abilene, 177

Harris Avenue Baptist Church (San Angelo, TX), 227, 229

Harris Hospital (Ft. Worth, TX), 212

Hawaii, 259

Hawkins, 154

Hawkins and I waited anxiously for the truck, 154

Headquarters Company, 147

Headquarters Company by awarding the company, 114

Headquarters Company of the 69th Engineer Battalion, 114

Headquarters Company, 326th Engineer Battalion (photo), 147

Headquarters Company, 69th Engineer Battalion, 115

Heard, Ann, 181

Heard, Pat, 181

Heath (Colleen) at the Concho Valley Vietnam Veterans Memorial (photo), 248

Heath left his mark at Goodfellow Air Force Base, 247

Heath, (Colleen) told me that I could visit, 231

Heath, Colleen, 231, 247

Heath, Colleen (photo), 248

Heath, James B. (paver), 247

Heath, James B. (photo), 247

heavy equipment at Fort Leonard Wood (photo), 60

Heavy Equipment Repairman, 58

Heavy Equipment Repairman (62B20), 238

Heavy Equipment Repairman Class (photo), 59

Heavy Equipment Repairman School, 62

Heller, Joseph, 104

Hendrick Medical Center in Abilene, 188

Hendricks Medical Center (Abilene, TX), 218

Hendricks Medical Center in Abilene, Texas, 223

Hereford, Texas, 46, 150

Hernandez, Robert, 22

Herndon (Capt. Robert L.) recommending me and some other, 154

Herndon, Cpt. Robert L., 154

HH1K, 136

HH1K, a Navy version of the Huey, 136

HHC, 326th Engineer Battalion, 146

HHC, 326th Engineer Battalion (Airmobile), 145

HHC, 326th Engineer Battalion, 101st Airborne Division (Airmobile), 159

Hill Fights, 240

Hillsboro, Texas, 198

history of Fort Campbell, Kentucky, 159

hit called, "PT-109", 17

Hiter, Capt. Thomas Y., 69

Hodgson, Ken, 227

Holland, 145

Holly, Buddy, 80

Holly's (Buddy) hit song, "That'll Be the Day", 80

Hollywood Jumps, 93

Honolulu, Hawaii, 259

Hooper, (Rev. Carrell) to discuss my planned, 213

Hooper, Rev. Carrell, 213

Hooper, Rev. Carrell (photo), 214

Hope (Bob) presented his Christmas Special to, 152

Hope (Bob) would perform at Camp Eagle, 152

Hope, Bob, 152, 153

Hopkinsville, Kentucky, 159

hospital chaplain, 187

Hovland, SP4, 114

HSU, 180, 182

HSU seemed like heaven on earth, 180

Hue during the Tet Offensive of 1968, 144

Hue, South Vietnam, 143, 144

Huey helicopter, 236

Huey, which came out of Fort Rucker, 236

Hueys, sometimes referred to as "Slicks.", 136

Hutchings, Terrance D., 54

Igo, (John) the Texas State Poet, 184

Igo, John, 184

In Flanders Field (poem), 15

Independence Day, 228

Indian from New Mexico, 150

Indiana, 128

Infantry School, 57, 58

Infiltration Course, 47

Inprocessing, 37

Inside the VC and the NVA (book), 126

Insignia of the 326th Engineer Battalion (image), 145

Institute of Heraldry, 113

Iowa Jima, 146

Iowa Jima ahead of the Marines, 146

Iran, 195

Iranian Crisis, 195

Iraq, 219, 234, 235

IV Corps area, 114

J. B. (dog), 138

J. B. (dog) credit for fathering the litter, 138

J. B. (dog) got his name from a CO, 137

J. B. (dog) had been with our outfit, 137

Index

J. J. (dog), 138

J. J. (dog) give birth to a litter of pups, 138

J. J. (dog) had been in-country, 138

J. J., (dog) which stood for "Janis Joplin", 138

J. J.'s litter and named her Mickey, 138

Janesville, Wisconsin, 240

Japan, 107, 109

Japanese, 192, 229

Japanese kamikaze planes, 32

Japanese on Java, 192

Japs, 19

Java, 192

Jennison, Barbara, 227

Jesus Christ, 163, 165, 166, 172, 173, 177, 178, 182, 183, 193, 198, 200, 238, 240, 244, 252

Jesus Christ –, 252

Jesus Christ as his Lord and Savior, 240

Jesus Christ as my Lord and Savior, 172

Jesus Christ as the real Jumpin' Jesus, 252

Jesus Christ had changed my life, 178

Jesus Christ is our best hope for, 193

Jesus Christ's death and resurrection, 164

Jesus would have kept my spirit, 252

Jesus' victory over death, 252

JFK, 17

Jimmy Dean sausage plant in Plainview, 17

Joe (movie), 106

Johnson, President Lyndon B. (photo), 13

Joplin, (Pastor Gene) the church (Bethel Bpt.) agreed to license me, 178

Joplin, Pastor Gene, 178

jump boots, 92

jump boots during a jump (photo), 199

jump from a C-141 Starlifter (photo), 191, 197

jump from a CH-47 Chinook (photo), 199

Jump Master in the sky, 254

Jump School, 1, 9, 11, 27, 57, 68, 72, 73, 82, 87, 88, 90, 111, 125, 126, 132, 169, 203

Jump School as the entrance into hell, 68

Jump School: Three Weeks at Hell's Gate, 67

Jump Week, 71, 90, 91, 96, 97

jumper gathers his parachute (photo), 10

Jumpin' Jesus, 85, 252

Jumping Jacks (movie), 80

Jumpmaster, 5, 6, 7, 8, 76

Jumpmaster, Jesus Christ, 165

Junell (Robert), our representative, 236

Junell, Robert, 236

Just for the Record (poem), 164

kamikaze pilots, 20

Kansas, 63, 220

Kansas City, Kansas, 220

Keeling, Randy (photo), 21

Kelly (Tom) carrying a framed copy, 220

Kelly said something in his book, 137

Kelly, (Tom) a school teacher, 218

Kelly, Daniel E., 134

Kelly, Tom, 218, 220

Kelly, Tom (photo), 219

Kelly, Tom, too, helped me minister, 218

Kelton, Elmer, 227

Kennedy, President John F., 13, 17

Kennedy, President John F. (photo), 13

Kennedy's (JFK) experiences as the commander of a, 17

Kentucky, 145, 159, 165, 169, 183, 186

Kentucky (photo), 175

Kentucky Colonels, 186

Kentucky Fried Chicken restaurant, 186

Kentucky while stationed at Fort Campbell, 186

Kerrville, Texas, 233

Khe Sanh in 1968, 240

Khe Sanh in the 1967 Hill Fights, 240

Khe Sanh was inside of a bowl, 240

Khe Sanh, South Vietnam, 240

Knoxville, Tennessee, 161

Kondo, Edward, 97

Korea, 20, 171

Korea (photo), 170

Korea in 1952, 171

Index

Korean War, 23, 24, 89, 106, 238

Koreans, 134

Krebs (Bill), flew Army transport airplanes (photo), 258

Krebs (Bill), flew C-46 and C-47 Army transports, 258

Krebs (Bill), on February 5, 1982, 259

Krebs (Bill), on the day of his last flight (photo), 259

Krebs (Pamela J.) became a better friend than, 181

Krebs, Bill, 257, 258, 259

Krebs, Bill (photo), 258, 259

Krebs, Pamela Jean, 181

Krebs, Pamela Jean (photo), 181

Ky Tek (village), 115, 124

Ky Tek, where six Viet Cong soldiers, 124

Lanning, Michael Lee, 126

Lawrence (Mayor Jay) greeted me, 226

Lawrence (Mayor Jay) greeted the author, 226

Lawrence, Mayor Jay, 226

Lawrence, Mayor Jay (photo), 226

Leadership Academy, 52, 55, 59

Leadership Academy (photo), 55

Leadership Academy at Fort Leonard Wood, 52

Leadership Academy at Fort Leonard Wood, Missouri (photo), 55

Leadership Academy at Fort Leonard, Missouri (photo), 51

Leadership Preparation Course (LPC), 52, 53, 54, 58, 59, 238

learning how to salute at Fort Ord (photo), 43

Leaving on a Jet Plane (song), 107

leaving the Army on August 21, 1973, 178

Lewis (Jerry) training on the towers, 80

Lewis, Jerry, 80

Lloyd, Lonnie, 220

LOH (light observation helicopter), 102

Lone Star State, 177

Long Binh, South Vietnam, 110, 111, 114

Long Thanh, 101

Long, Albert, 127

Long, Albert (photo), 130

Lord used Bro. Terry, 187

Lord, here I come!, 252

Los Angeles, California, 35

Lost-in-the-Woods Leadership, 52

Lost-in-the-Woods, Misery, 54

Louisiana, 238

LST, 152

LST along the coast of Vietnam, 152

Lubbock, Texas, 8, 35, 103, 106

Luchino, Gerald T., 113

M.A.S.H. (movie), 106

M-16, 154

M-16 on full automatic and fired, 140

M-16 rifle, 46, 117, 124, 140, 153

M-16 rifle (photo), 36

M-16A1, 46

M-60 machine gun, 124, 125, 154, 197, 221

M-60 machine gun (photo), 196

M-60 machine guns, 196

M-60 was changing the barrel, 197

M72 LAW, 46

M79 Grenade Launcher, 46

Mac, 117

Mac out at the barge, 117

Mac took me to a barge area, 117

Mac wanted to scare me since, 117

Mair about Warren's life, 201

Mair, George, 200

marching, 41

Marine Corps Recon, 134

Marines, 81, 82, 146, 218, 240

Martin, Dean, 80

Mason, Dr. Zane, 180

Mason's (Dr. Zane) history tests, 180

Massy-Ferguson 410 Combine, 63

Master of Divinity degree, 211

Mathis Field (San Angelo, TX), 234, 236

Matthews (W. F.) into its Hall of Fame, 238

Matthews (W. F.) with his wife, Gladys (photo), 229

Matthews, (W. F.) had survived 3 ½ years as a prisoner of war, 229

Matthews, (W. F.) who survived 3 ½ years, 192

Matthews, Gladys (photo), 229

Index

Matthews, W. F., 192, 229, 230, 238

Matthews, W. F. (photo), 229

Matthews, W. F. for induction into the Southwest, 230

Matthews, W. F. too had joined the Texas Army National Guard, 192

McBride, Terry, 127

McBride, Terry (photo), 128

McCain (John S.) managed to escape, 18

McCain, (John S.) a Navy pilot, 18

McCain, Senator John S., 18

McCain's (John S.) A-4 Skyhawk, 18

McClintock, SP4, 114

McCormick, William, 150

McCoy (Mike) and some of the other, 173

McCoy (Mike) and the Navigators, 172

McCoy, Judy, 166

McCoy, Mike, 166, 172, 173

McCoy, Mike started teaching me how to, 166

McCoy. Mike and his wife, Judy, 166

McCrae, John, 15

McCrae's concept of the dead, 15

McCullough replied with one word: "Nuts!", 144

McCullough, General, 144

McDowell (Danny) and Dickie ("Duke") Crowder, spent most of, 100

McDowell (Danny) offered me lots of words of encouragement, 151

McDowell (Danny) took me to West Texas University, 103

McDowell, (Danny) I made trips to other, 103

McDowell, Danny, 100, 103, 151

McDowell, Danny (photo), 103

McFarland, Ronald, 150

McKinnon, Robert, 180

McMurray University (Abilene, TX), 231

McNally, SP4, 114

McSwain, Ross, 227

Medal-of-Honor, 51

meeting place for Vietnam Veterans of America (photo), 234

Mekong Delta, 112, 114, 120, 125, 147, 148, 150

Mekong Delta (photo), 116

Mekong Delta a tropical paradise, 120

Mekong Delta of South Vietnam (photo), 130

Mekong Princess (poem), 125

Memorial Day, 227, 228, 232, 234

Memorial Day ceremony, 234

Memorial Day, Vasquez (Armando) and Bright (Tom), 232

Mercer Island Baptist Church, 182

Mercer Island Baptist Church (Mercer Island, WA), 187

Mercer Island, Washington, 182

Merkel, Texas, 231

Mexico, 159, 186

Michigan, 53, 62

Mickey (puppy), 138, 221

Mickey (puppy) didn't last long, 138

Mickey (puppy) who shared my war, 221

Mickey, (puppy) in South Vietnam (photo), 138

Middleton, (Sheriff A. C.) who attended our church faithfully, 187

Middleton, Sheriff A. C., 187

military chaplain, 201

military chaplaincy, 194

military occupational speciality (MOS), 58

military occupational specialty (MOS), 58, 111, 238

Military Regions III and IV, 112

Minister of Music and Youth, 187

Minister of Youth, 187, 188

Miss America, 153

missionary trips to Vietnam, 240

Missouri, 51, 52, 55, 60, 61, 63, 238, 239

Mitchell (Billy) pushed for the development, 68

Mitchell, Billy, 68

Mitton, John, 181

Mitton, John (photo), 180

Mitton, John and I became a two-man ministry team, 181

Mitton, John and I roomed together, 181

Monday (Arthur) had served against the British, 162

Monday (Dean) served with the Navy Seabees, 146

Monday (Jared) at Texoma Medical Center (photo), 215

Index 301

Monday (Jared) glides to earth under a parachute (photo), 261

Monday (Jared) in San Angelo (photo), 257

Monday (Jared) right after his skydiving (photo), 265

Monday (Jared) with his grandfather, Bill Krebs (photo), 258

Monday (Joe) made a career out of, 19

Monday (Joe) served with the Navy Seawolves (photo), 134

Monday (Le'Ann) with Pam Monday on (photo), 264

Monday (Malchi) became a prisoner of war, 161

Monday (Pam) had to wait until May, 1978, 188

Monday (Pam) in Harris Hospital (photo), 212

Monday (Pam) in the sky over Stanton (photo), 263

Monday (Pam) on the day (photo), 264

Monday (Pam) on the day of the family (photo), 264

Monday (Pam) prepares to make a parachute jump (photo), 263

Monday (Pam) with her mother, Ellie (photo), 190

Monday (Shelby & Malchi) served the Confederacy, 160

Monday (Shelby Y.) and his brother Malchi served with, 160

Monday (Tim) immediately following his jump (photo), 265

Monday (Tim) prepares to land (photo), 262

Monday (Tim), Le'Ann (Tim's wife), and Pam Monday (photo), 264

Monday (Travis & Pam) during their college days (photo), 189

Monday (Travis & Pam) on their wedding day (photo), 189

Monday (Travis) and Bob Dils jokingly point to a sign (photo), 133

Monday (Travis) and Martin Green (photo), 48

Monday (Travis) arrives back in the United States (photo), 157

Monday (Travis) at Fort Benning, Georgia (photo), 70

Monday (Travis) at Redbird Drop Zone in Dallas (photo), 250

Monday (Travis) at Tan Hoa (photo), 129

Monday (Travis) at the Leadership Academy (photo), 55

Monday (Travis) back at home in Plainview, Texas (photo), 64

Monday (Travis) drove around in this contact truck (photo), 175

Monday (Travis) gives Private Currie a lift (photo), 55

Monday (Travis) in front of his tent (photo), 121

Monday (Travis) in his home in Colorado City, 246

Monday (Travis) in Jump School (photo), 1

Monday (Travis) in San Angelo, Texas (photo), 237

Monday (Travis) in the back of a 5-ton (photo), 156

Monday (Travis) in the motor pool (photo), 128

Monday (Travis) in the push up position (photo), 36

Monday (Travis) on the campus (photo), 190

Monday (Travis) practices hand-to-hand combat (photo), 48

Monday (Travis) standing in front (photo), 174

Monday (Travis) taken while he was enroute (photo), 157

Monday (Travis) waits to board a C-141 (photo), 207

Monday (Travis) while with the 143d Airborne Infantry(photo), 255

Monday (Travis) with Bob Dils at Binh Thuy North (photo), 142

Monday (Travis) with Colleen Heath (photo), 248

Monday (Travis) with Edward Arnold and James Robb (photo), 53

Monday (Travis) with family members in Plainview (photo), 104

Monday (Travis) with his best friend at Hardin-Simmons (photo), 180

Monday (Travis) with his brother, Derrell (photo), 33

Monday (Travis) with his mother, Wilma (photo), 28

Monday (Travis) with his son, Jared (photo), 245

Monday (Travis), during his senior year (photo), 33

Monday (Travis), in Plainview, Texas (photo), 103

Monday boys, 186

Monday family in Colorado City, Texas (photo), 245

Monday in a UH-1B helicopter (photo), 209

Monday in Can Tho (photo), 113

Monday in his barracks (photo), 165

Monday in his khaki uniform (photo), 166

Index

Monday in Vietnam (photo), 142

Monday married in Mercer Island (photo), 182

Monday relatives had fought there, 160

Monday relatives had migrated, 162

Monday, (Dean) who served in the Navy, 146

Monday, (Jared Daniel) in Texoma Medical Center in Denison, Texas, 215

Monday, (Joe) helped fight the fires, 18

Monday, (Joe) made a career, 17

Monday, (Joe) the one who served on the USS Forrestal, 134

Monday, (Joe) who made a career, 146

Monday, (Joe) worked out of Binh Thuy Naval Base, 111

Monday, (Pam) completed her studies in December, 1977, 188

Monday, (Travis) a jet-jumpin' paratrooper (photo), 208

Monday, Arthur, 162

Monday, Dean, 146

Monday, Dean (photo), 146

Monday, Derrell, 105, 150, 163, 177, 213, 222

Monday, Derrell (photo), 30, 33, 163

Monday, Derrell accepted my invitation, 213

Monday, Derrell also corresponded with me, 105

Monday, Derrell took guitar lessons, 150

Monday, Derrell, a Baptist minister, had been trying, 163

Monday, Derrell, and asked him to preach my ordination, 213

Monday, Derrell, who had surrendered to God's call, 105

Monday, Derrell's help, I gained acceptance into, 177

Monday, Henry, 161

Monday, Henry who later fought for the Union, 161

Monday, Janelle, 136

Monday, Jared also flew in a glider, 258

Monday, Jared Daniel, 215, 222, 257, 258, 261, 262

Monday, Jared Daniel (photo), 215, 257, 258, 261, 265

Monday, Jared had a real good experience, 262

Monday, Jared made the first jump, 262

Monday, Jared, at a veterans' event (photo), 245

Monday, Jared's birth also filled my heart, 215

Monday, Joe, 17, 18, 19, 31, 111, 134, 135, 136, 137, 146

Monday, Joe (photo), 19, 30, 31, 134, 135

Monday, Joe also spoke of flying in an HH1K, 136

Monday, Joe and I got together in Vietnam, 135

Monday, Joe if he served as a door gunner, 136

Monday, Joe into letting me record an interview, 135

Monday, Joe on the internet, 137

Monday, Joe told me the following story, 136

Monday, Joe, now don't you go and die, 136

Monday, Joe's powerful laugh, 137

Monday, Jr. (W. B.) with his mother, Gladys (photo), 31

Monday, Jr. (W. B.), with his brother and sister (photo), 30

Monday, Jr. (W. B.), with his son, Derrell (photo), 30

Monday, Jr., (W. B.) met me at the airport, 106

Monday, Jr., (W. B.) taught me to shoot, 46

Monday, Jr., (W. B.) went to school with Jimmy, 16

Monday, Jr., (W. B.) who graduated from Plainview High School (photo), 16

Monday, Juanita (photo), 30, 31

Monday, Le'Ann, 262

Monday, Le'Ann (photo), 264

Monday, Lee (photo), 146

Monday, Malchi, 160, 161

Monday, Malchi and Shelby had a younger brother, 161

Monday, Nelda, 146

Monday, Pam added to the excitement of, 212

Monday, Pam and I both faced times of great difficulty, 215

Monday, Pam and I found it easy, 187

Monday, Pam and I had relocated to San Angelo, Texas, 227

Monday, Pam and I moved to Fort Worth, Texas, 188

Monday, Pam and Jared (Monday) also attended the school, 222

Monday, Pam did not get to attend my graduation, 212

Index

Monday, Pam finished in December of that, 187

Monday, Pam found a job working for Olmstead Kirk Paper Company, 188

Monday, Pam has been wonderful, 213

Monday, Pam if I could interview her, 260

Monday, Pam is still the best person that, 182

Monday, Pam jumped after Tim, 262

Monday, Pam knew how depressed I felt, 214

Monday, Pam rode in the cockpit, 259

Monday, Pam screaming, "You kicked me!", 216

Monday, Pam surprised me one day, 260

Monday, Pam to graduate from HSU, 188

Monday, Pam told our sons, Tim and Jared, 261

Monday, Pam: I plan to go skydiving, 261

Monday, Pamela (Krebs), 187, 188, 191, 198, 200, 212, 213, 214, 215, 216, 222, 252, 257, 259, 260, 261, 262

Monday, Pamela (Krebs) (photo), 182, 189, 190, 212, 214, 215, 257, 263, 264

Monday, Shelby Y., 160, 161

Monday, Shelby, after sustaining a wound, 161

Monday, Sr., (W. B.) spent most of his adult life as a barber (photo), 29

Monday, Sr., (W. B.) the author's grandfather (photo), 29

Monday, Sr., (W. B.) told me about riding horseback, 17

Monday, Tim and his wife Le'Ann joined us, 262

Monday, Tim attended high school, 259

Monday, Tim introduced me in a school assembly, 220

Monday, Tim jumped next, 262

Monday, Tim spent many hours at their house, 213

Monday, Timothy William, 212, 213, 215, 220, 222, 257, 259, 261, 262

Monday, Timothy William (photo), 212, 214, 215, 257, 259, 260, 264, 265

Monday, Travis, 13, 35, 72, 92, 98, 143, 175, 211

Monday, Travis (photo), 1, 21, 28, 33, 36, 48, 49, 53, 55, 64, 70, 103, 104, 105, 113, 121, 128, 129, 130, 133, 142, 156, 157, 163, 165, 166, 174, 180, 182, 189, 190, 207, 208, 209, 214, 215, 219, 237, 245, 246, 248, 250, 257

Monday, Travis hated K. P., 43

Monday, Travis volunteered for a two-week Leadership, 52

Monday, Travis, Pam, Tim, and Jared in San Angelo (photo), 257

Monday, W. B., Jr., 17, 46, 106

Monday, W. B., Jr. (photo), 16, 30, 135

Monday, W. B., Jr. and I, along with some, 106

Monday, W. B., Sr., 17, 106

Monday, W. B., Sr. (photo), 29

Monday's (Travis) graduation photo from Basic Training, 49

Monday's (Travis) little puppy, Mickey (photo), 138

Monde, (Major Bennet B.) author of the book, 224

Monde, Major Bennet B., 224

Monterey Bay, 37

Monterey in the war with Mexico, 159

Monterey Peninsula, 36

Monterey, Mexico, 159

Montgomery (Charles) and I made several trips, 105

Montgomery, Charles, 105

Montgomery, Charles (photo), 105

Monument, Colorado, 258

Moore, Robin, 25

Morton (Randy) served his country in both, 26

Morton, Randy, 26

MOS of Heavy Equipment Repairman (62B20), 238

MOS would be 62B10, 58

motor pool -- a graveyard, 117

motor pool at Tan Hoa (photo), 118

motto of the 34th Engineer Group, 114

motto: "Building Combat Power", 113

movie, *The Alamo*, 25

movie, *The Green Berets*, 25

Moving Wall, 231, 232, 239

Moving Wall at San Angelo's Goodfellow Air Force Base, 231

Moving Wall in Big Spring, Texas, 232

Moving Wall on the campus of Angelo State University, 231

Moving Wall on the campus of McMurray University, 231

Moving Wall that is at ASU, 238

Moving Wall to visit San Angelo (TX), 231

Munoz, Bobby, 181

Index

Naff, Ellie (photo), 190

Nam Vet: Making Peace with Your Past (book), 217

NASA's Texas Fly High Program, 259, 260

Nashville, Tennessee, 161

National Guard, 61, 195, 204, 250

National Guard Airborne Ranger unit, 253

National Guard Armory (San Angelo, TX), 236

National Guard Armory in Hillsboro, Texas, 198

National Guard Armory there in Arlington (TX), 201

National Guard drills, 205

National Moment of Remembrance, 228

Nationalist Chinese, 168

Navigators, 166, 172, 173

Navy, 127, 146

Navy Seabees, 146

Navy Seabees in World War II, 146

Navy SEAL, 140

Navy SEALs, 134

Navy Seawolves, 134

Navy Seawolves in Vietnam, 134

Navy version of the UH-1B helicopter (photo), 136

Neighbors, Jim, 153

New Guinea (photo), 258

New Jersey, 167

New Mexico, 150

New York World Fair in 1939, 80

Nichols (John S.) of California, who flew with Steve, 229

Nichols (John) about Steve in Vietnam, 102

Nichols, (John S.) who served in Vietnam with Steve, 101

Nichols, (John S.) who shares my desire to honor, 229

Nichols, John S., 101, 102, 229

Nichols, John S. and Steve flew together, 102

Nichols, John S. for telling me about his service, 102

Nichols, John sent me via email, 102

Niemann, Judy, 227

Nineteen Jumps and a Prayer (book), 250

Nixon, President Richard, 151

Nixon, President Richard M., 169

Nixon's (President Richard M.) decision to get most of our troops, 151

Nixon's (President Richard M.) major troop withdrawals, 169

noncommissioned officers (NCOs), 72

Normandy, 145

North Carolina, 91, 112, 113, 150, 162

North Vietnamese Army (NVA), 126, 153, 154

North Vietnamese soldiers had overrun, 116

NVA and the VC were the bad guys, 126

O.D. Blues (poem), 132

O.D. green, 132

Oakland Army Base, California, 97, 106, 107

Oakland, California, 106, 107

Odessa, Texas, 24

officers in Vocational Industrial Clubs of America (photo), 21

OH-6a LOH, 102

Ohio, 237

OJT, 117

Okinawa, 168

Oklahoma, 212, 213, 214, 215, 217

Oklahoma, during late summer in 1981, 212

Oldfather, Teressa (Monday), 17, 62

Oldfather, Teressa (Monday) (photo), 104

Oldfather, Teressa, in Plainview, Texas (photo), 33

Oldfather, Teressa's (Monday) birthday, 62

Olmstead Kirk Paper Company, 188

Operation Desert Shield, 219

Operation Desert Storm, 219

Ord, (Gen. Edward Cresap) who served as a lieutenant, 36

Ord, Gen. Edward Cresap, 36

Otto Carter Story, 231

Outpost Director of Point Man International Ministries, 218

Outstanding Auto Mechanics Chapter of Texas, 22

Outstanding Soldier of the Month, 167

Outstanding VICA Student of Texas, 22

OV-10 Broncos, 122

Overstreet, Johnny, 106

Index

Owens (John G.) from North Carolina, 150

Owens (John G.) got called out to the bunker line, 151

Owens (John G.) on generators, 151

Owens, (John G.) the guy teaching me, 150

Owens, John G., 150, 151

P.O.W. experiences, 229

P.T. (physical training), 72

P-47 Thunderbolt, 230, 231

P-47 Thunderbolts (photo), 230

Pacific Lutheran College in Tacoma, Washington, 182

Pacific Ocean, 17, 19, 107, 258

Pacific Theater, 32

Palmer (Captain) disapproved them all, 133

Palmer, Captain, 133

Pampa, Texas, 146

Pampa, Texas, with his wife, Nelda, 146

pamphlet given to Travis Monday (image), 249

panhandle of Texas, 61

Parachute Landing Falls (PLF), 73

Parachute Landing Falls (PLFs), 73, 76, 82, 96, 200, 254

paratroopers of the 143d Airborne Infantry (photo), 206

Parker, Fess, 25

Parlow, Patrick, 150

Parrott, (Joshua) interviewed me in my home, 228

Parrott, Joshua, 228

Parrott's (Joshua) article, 228

pastor, 213

pastor of Calvary Baptist Church (Colorado City, TX), 215

pastor of Harris Avenue Baptist Church (San Angelo, TX), 227

pastor of Trinity Baptist Church (Sweetwater, TX), 222, 223

pastor of Yuba Baptist Church (Yuba, OK), 212, 213

patch of the 101st Airborne Division (photo), 143

patch of the 173d Airborne Brigade (photo), 168

patch of the 20th Engineer Brigade, 112

patch of the 20th Engineer Brigade (photo), 112

patch of the 36th Infantry Division, 193

patch of the 82nd Airborne Division (photo), 194

patriot, 25

patriotic Americans, 26

patriotic spirit, 15, 17

patriotic tendencies, 17

patriotism, 14, 25, 105, 219

patrol boats riverine, 134

Patton, Gen. George, 167

Patton's Third Army, 167

Paul the Apostle, 177

paver (for Elias Torrez, III) (photo), 235

Paver honoring James B. Heath, 247

PBRs, 134, 135

PBRs (patrol boats riverine), 134

Peck, Gregory, 23

perfectly good airplane, 1, 89, 261

perfectly good airplanes, 263

Perkins, Jack, 218

Perry, Gladys (photo), 163

Perry, Gladys (Young), 135

Perry, Gladys (Young) (photo), 31

Peter, Paul, and Mary, 107

Philadelphia Eagles, 21

Phillips (holding puppy) and Travis Monday (photo), 142

Phillips, Bobby, 127

Phillips, Bobby (photo), 142

Phillips, came over with the U. S. Navy, 127

Phillips, N. G., 20

Phillips, N. G. (photo), 104

Phillips, Wilma (William) and Glynn (Phillips) wanted to take, 64

Phillips, Wilma (Williams), 19, 27, 35, 64, 94, 99, 120, 150, 152, 173

Phillips, Wilma (Williams) (photo), 28, 104

Phillips, Wilma (Williams) would be there for me, 99

Phillips, Wlima (Williams), 40

Phu Bai area, 150, 155

Phu Bai Fever (poem), 153

Phu Bai, South Vietnam, 143, 147, 150, 155

Physical Education (P. E.), 21

Physical Recreation, 188

Pioneer City-County Museum, 103

Pioneer Museum (Sweetwater, TX), 224, 230

Pioneer Parachute Company, 86

Plainview City Cemetery, 179

Plainview City Cemetery in Plainview, Texas (photo), 179

Plainview High School, 20, 21, 26, 28, 33, 58, 62, 101, 127

Plainview High School Band, 41

Plainview High School in Plainview, Texas, 16, 228

Plainview patriots, 26

Plainview sports experience, 20

Plainview, Texas, 15, 16, 17, 20, 22, 24, 25, 26, 28, 29, 33, 39, 64, 99, 100, 101, 106, 117, 133, 150, 151, 157, 159, 177, 178, 179, 228, 231

Plainview, Texas (photo), 103, 104, 178

PLF, 10, 198

poem about God's forgiveness, 164

poem by John McCrae, 15

poem called, "Among the Dead", 117

poem called, "O.D. Blues", 132

poem called, "Returning", 183

poem called, "The Ballad of the Basic Combat Trainee", 37

poem, called "Phu Bai Fever", 153

poem, called "Vietnam Romance", 184

poem. I called it, "Mekong Princess", 125

Point Man, 216

Point Man as an outpost leader, 218

Point Man International Ministries, 218

Point Man Ministries, 217, 218

Poison Ivy (song), 41

Pork Chop Hill (movie), 23

Post Traumatic Stress Disorder (PTSD), 183, 184, 214, 215, 216, 217, 222, 229, 243, 244

Prairie View Baptist Church (Anson, TX), 187

Presidential Unit Citations, 145

Prevail Through Surrendering Daily (PTSD), 244

price of freedom, 242

Price, Brooks (Seigler), 228

Priest (Coach) led us through an, 20

priest remained in-country with those orphans, 154

Priest, Coach, 20

Private Life of Sherlock Holmes (movie), 104

PT boat, 17

PT-109 (song), 17

PTSD reminds me to Prevail Through, 244

publication *Reveille*, 216

Pulaski County, Missouri, 51

Purple Heart, 38, 110, 111

Purple Pups (football team), 20

qualifying jump, 97

Quang Tin Province, 116

Quevera, Che, 171

quick-release mechanism, 83

Quintanilla, Tom, 22

Rangel (Rudy) enabled me to take a handoff, 20

Rangel, Rudy, 20

Ranger camp and firebase, 115

Ranger School, 58

Rapedo Drop Zone, 204

rats at Camp Wilkinson, 148

Reception Center, 38

Reception Center (Fort Ord), 37

Red Pups (football team), 20

Redbird Drop Zone, 204

Redbird Drop Zone in Dallas, 198

Redbird Drop Zone in Dallas, Texas (photo), 199, 250

Regular Army, 60, 61

Republic of South Vietnam, 92, 168, 183, 219

reserve parachutes, 74

Returning (poem), 183

Reveille (publication), 216

revenge for what they did to, 126

Rhea County, Tennessee, 162

Richardson (Gene) chose to leave, 253

Richardson (Gene) wrote a moving good-bye, 253

Richardson, (Sgt. Gene) suffered a similar injury, 203

Richardson, Sgt. Gene, 203, 253, 254

Richardson, Sgt. Gene (photo), 253

Richardson, Sgt. Gene replied, "I think I may have broken my leg, too", 203

Richardson, Sgt. Gene said, "Monday, is that you?", 203

rifle ranges, 44

Ripcord (T.V. show), 14

Index

river crossing in Arkansas (photo), 209

river patrol boats, 135

Roach, Edward, 222

Robb (James) agreed to join me, 62

Robb (James) and I also had a hard time, 60

Robb (James) and I had hoped, 60

Robb (James) and I returned to the barracks, 61

Robb (James) and I, both graduates of LPC, 59

Robb (James) and me a hard time, 61

Robb (James) and me consisted of animosity, 60

Robb (James) got the job of class leader, 60

Robb (James) handled the cold better, 62

Robb (James) of Michigan, 53

Robb (James) with Travis Monday at the Leadership Academy (photo), 55

Robb, James, 53, 59, 60, 61, 62, 97

Robb, James (photo), 53, 55

Robbins, Marty, 25

Rodgers (Lorraine Zillner) believes that she survived, 225

Rodgers (Lorraine Zillner) during WASP 2000, 226

Rodgers (Lorraine Zillner) gave me the best, 225

Rodgers (Lorraine, Zillner) still believed in both parachutes and prayer, 226

Rodgers, Lorraine Zillner, 225, 226

Rodgers, Lorraine Zillner (photo), 225

Rodriquez (Alberto) of Kerrville, Texas, 233

Rodriquez, Alberto, 233

Roever (Dave) out of Forth Worth, Texas, 240

Roever, Dave, 240

Rolfe (Meredith) when she fell out of, 86

Rolfe, WASP Cadet Meredith, 86

Rotary Club (Sweetwater), 260

Rotary Club (Sweetwater, TX), 223

ROTC program at Hardin Simmons, 179

Rucker, Ronald C., 54

runs at Fort Benning (photo), 81

Saddleback Church in California, 200

Sadler, Barry, 25

Saigon to Da Nang by C-130, 143

Saigon, South Vietnam, 111, 143

San Angelo called Concho Valley Vietnam Veterans, 233

San Angelo had seen a Veterans Day Parade, 241

San Angelo Museum of Fine Arts, 230

San Angelo native Fess Parker, 25

San Angelo schools let out, 242

San Angelo Standard-Times (newspaper), 234

San Angelo, Texas, 25, 161, 227, 229, 230, 231, 232, 233, 234, 236, 237, 239, 240, 241, 247, 248, 257

San Antonio, Texas, 25

San Francisco, California, 36, 259

Sanchez, 150

Sanders, Colonel, 186

Sands, John, 166

Savage (Cleo) helped instill, 22

Savage, Cleo, 22, 58, 62

Savage, Cleo (photo), 21

Savage's (Cleo) Auto Mechanics Class, 62

Savage's (Cleo) excellent teaching in Auto Mechanics, 58

say repeatedly, "Airborne! Airmobile! Airbubble!", 144

Screaming Eagles, 141, 143, 144, 145, 169

Screaming Eagles at Bastogne, 145

Screaming Eagles' famous stand, 144

Seabees, 146

Seabees in World War II, 146

SEALs, 135, 136

Seawolves, 111, 134, 135, 137

Seawolves in Vietnam, 134

Seawolves of HA(L)-3, 134

Seawolves was a good-humored outfit, 137

Seawolves: First Choice (book), 134

Secretary of the Army, 114

Seigler (Steve) and I did not know, 100

Seigler (Steve) for the church newsletter, 228

Seigler (Steve) had died in Vietnam, 99

Seigler (Steve) in his "hooch" in Vietnam (photo), 107

Seigler (Steve) in Vietnam (photo), 101

Seigler (Steve) in Vietnam with his (photo), 108

Seigler (Steve) liked the song "Leaving on a Jet Plane", 107

Seigler (Steve) shortly before I entered the Army, 107

Seigler, (Dr. Gale) had given me physicals, 100

Seigler, (Steve) who, like me, graduated from, 228

Seigler, Betty, 101

Seigler, Dr. Gale, 100, 101

Seigler, Steve, 26, 99, 100, 102, 107, 179, 221, 228, 229, 231

Seigler, Steve (photo), 100, 101, 107, 108

Seigler, Steve (tribute to), 102

Seigler, Steve died in Bien Hoa, 102

Seigler, Steve in Vietnam, 229

Seigler, Steve was one of those brave men, 102

Seigler, Steve's sister, Brooks Seigler Price, 228

Seigler, Steve's tour of duty in Vietnam, 102

Seigler's (Dr. Gale) wife and Steve's mother, Betty, 101

Seigler's (Steve) death intensified my, 102

Seigler's (Steve) family in Plainview (TX), 228

Seigler's grave in Plainview City Cemetery, 179

Seminary Sunday School Department, 200

September 11, 2001, 226

September 11, 2001, attacks, 226

serve the Lord as a hospital chaplain, 187

Seth Ward, 15, 17

shoulder patch of the 173d Airborne Brigade (photo), 168

shoulder patch of the 82nd Airborne Division (photo), 194

Siege of Khe Sanh in 1968, 240

Siege of the Alamo (song), 25

silver wings of a paratrooper, 111

silver wings of the U. S. Army paratrooper, 89

Silverton, Texas, 103

Sisemore, (Jerry) who later played professional, 21

Sisemore, Jerry, 21

Six Flags Over Texas, 79

Sky Soldiers, 159, 167, 168, 169

Sky Soldiers endured almost six years, 168

Sky Soldiers of the former 173ᵈ, 159

skydiving, 6, 14, 261, 262

Slicks, 136

Slip away!, 10

Smith, Governor Preston, 22

Smith, Russell S., 227

soldier of Jesus Christ, 177

song "Leaving on a Jet Plane", 107

song called "Blood on the Risers", 2

song, "Ballad of the Green Berets, 25

song, "Big John", 17

song, "Siege of the Alamo", 25

song, "That'll Be the Day", 80

song, "You've Got a Friend.", 151

songs was "Leaving on a Jet Plane", 107

Sound off for equipment check!, 7

South America, 171

South Carolina, 145

South Vietnam, 90, 92, 102, 109, 113, 138, 183, 219

South Vietnam (photo), 116, 130

South Vietnamese, 23

Southcliff Baptist Church (Fort Worth, TX, 200

Southwest Military Museum (San Angelo, TX), 238, 239

Southwest Military Museum Hall of Fame (San Angelo, TX), 230

Southwestern Baptist Theological Seminary, 211

Southwestern Baptist Theological Seminary (Fort Worth, TX), 188, 211, 222

Spade Ranch south of Colorado City, Texas, 186

Spear, Ted, 181

Special Forces, 57, 58

Specials Forces, 38

Spector(Ronald H.) says, "Rats were a constant nuisance", 148

Spector, Ronald H., 148

spirit of Airborne, 71

squadron, DF11, 19

squadron, DF74, 19

Stand in the door!, 7

stand-up landings, 73

Stanton, author of *Vietnam Order of Battle*, 110

Stanton, Shelby L., 110

Stanton, Texas, 262, 263

Stanton, Texas, for an adventure in skydiving, 262

State of Wisconsin, 240

States, 65, 109

static line, 3

static line jumps, 6, 90

static lines, 6

statue of infantryman at Fort Benning, Georgia (photo), 68

Stevens (H. B.) a plaque with Rolfe's name, 86

Stevens (H. B.) went from selling sewing, 86

Stevens, H. B., 86

stick, 8

Student Brigade (Airborne), 69

Summers, Capt. J. B., 137

Suspended Agony, 82

Suspended Harness, 82

Sweetwater (TX) for five and a half years, 222

Sweetwater City Commission, 226

Sweetwater High School, 259

Sweetwater High School students (photo), 260

Sweetwater Reporter (newspaper), 224

Sweetwater Rotary Club, 260

Sweetwater Swatter (P-47) (photo), 230

Sweetwater, Texas, 86, 103, 222, 223, 224, 225, 226, 230, 246, 259, 260

Sweetwater, Texas, Mayor Jay Lawrence (photo), 226

Sweetwater's Avenger Field, 224

Swing Landing Trainer, 82

symbol or patch for VVA 457, 243

T-10, 90, 96, 204

T-10 main parachute, 96

T-10 military parachute, 90

T-10 sported a 28-foot canopy, 90

T-4, 90

Tacoma, Washington, 182

Takaki, Gene, 180

Tam Ky in Quang Tin Province, 116

Tan Hoa, 115, 117, 119, 138, 238

Tan Hoa (photo), 109, 116, 118, 121, 128, 129, 130

Tan Hoa in the Mekong Delta (photo), 130

Tan Hoa stood next to a highway, 115

Tan Hoa was about the size of, 115

Tan Hoa, south of Binh Thuy and Can Tho (photo), 116

Taylor, James, 151

Temple Baptist Church (Abilene, TX), 187

Temple Baptist Church of Abilene, 188

Tennessee, 159, 160, 161, 162, 177

tent at Tan Hoa (photo), 121

Tent City, 115

Terry (Rev. H. B.) learned that Pam didn't, 187

Terry (Rev. H. B.) to help prepare me, 187

Terry, Faye, 187

Terry, Jr., and his wife, Faye, 187

Terry, Rev. H. B, Jr., 187

Terry's (Rev. H. B.) strengths included hospital and grief, 187

Test Platoon, 68, 69, 80

Tet Offensive of 1968, 114, 144

Texan, 193

Texans, 36, 38

Texas, 5, 8, 14, 15, 16, 22, 24, 33, 35, 39, 46, 61, 63, 79, 80, 86, 90, 99, 103, 111, 114, 141, 146, 149, 150, 161, 180, 186, 187, 188, 191, 198, 199, 211, 215, 218, 220, 222, 223, 227, 228, 231, 232, 233, 236, 239, 245, 257, 259, 262

Texas Army National Guard, 45, 188, 191, 192, 193, 196, 197, 201, 204, 211, 250, 251, 255

Texas Chute-Out, 79

Texas flag, 261

Texas Fly High Program, 259, 260

Texas History (class), 25

Texas pride, 44

Texas Sports Hall of Fame Museum, 21

Texas State Poet, 184

Texas T Patch of the 36th Infantry Division, 193

Texas troops at Goliad, 24

Texas War of Independence, 24

Texoma Medical Center in Denison, Texas, 215

That'll Be the Day (song), 80

The Alamo (movie), 25

Index

The Corral (college magazine), 185

The Green Berets (book), 25

The Green Berets (movie), 25

The Purpose Driven Life (book), 200

The Task is Ours, 145

Third Army, 167

Thirty Years of Sausage, Fifty Years of Ham (book), 16

Thompson (Mike) as president, 22

Thompson, (Oscar) more than anyone else, 201

Thompson, (Oscar) taught a class on, 201

Thompson, Carolyn, 201

Thompson, Mike (photo), 21

Thompson, Oscar, 201

Thompson, Oscar's insights quite helpful, 201

Thompson's (Oscar) emphasis on building, 201

Thorn, Dr. W. E. ("Bill"), 227

Together in war; together in peace (motto), 243

Tom Green County Courthouse (San Angelo, TX), 232

Torres (Elias), III, who had recently died in Iraq, 234

Torres, Elias, III, 234

Torrez (Elias), III, who died in action, 235

Torrez, Elias, III, 235

Tower Week, 71, 88

towers at Fort Benning, 79, 81

trainees had to learn how to make up their bunks (photo), 42

training jump at Fort Benning (photo), 93

Travis (William Barrett) prepared a last desperate, 24

Travis and the other Alamo defenders, 122

Travis Avenue Baptist Church (Ft. Worth, TX), 212

Travis, (William Barrett) commander of the Alamo, 187

Travis, (William Barrett) the commander of the Alamo, 24

Travis, Col. William Barrett, 122, 187

Travis, Colonel William Barrett, 24

Travis, commander of the Alamo, 122

Trinity Baptist Church (Sweetwater, TX), 222, 223, 246

TRP I, 3d SQDN, 163d ARMD CAV REGT, 250

Twilight Zone (TV show), 109

Twin-Vue Drive-In Theater (Plainview), TX), 25

Tyler, Chaplain Milton, 187

U .S. Flag, 228

U. S. Air Force, 247

U. S. Army, 26, 58

U. S. Army Engineer Command, Vietnam, 113

U. S. Army Engineers, 58

U. S. Army, Vietnam (USARV), 110

U. S. Army's Airborne School, 1

U. S. Army's first paratrooper units, 68

U. S. Navy, 17, 19

U.S. Army in Korea, 20

U.S. flags on graves at the cemeteries, 216

U.S.A., 186

UH-1B, 209

UH-1B helicopter (photo), 136

UH-1B helicopter over Fort Chaffee (photo), 209

UH-1B Hueys, sometimes referred to as "Slicks", 136

UH-B1 medevac helicopter, 125

Uncle Sam, 27, 132

Union, 160, 161

Union Army, 161

Union in E Company of the 10th Cavalry, 161

Union troops to victory, 160

United States of America, 14, 90, 119, 131, 155, 157, 221

USS Alpine, 20

USS Alpine (photo), 32

USS Forrestal, 17, 134

USS Forrestal (photo), 18, 31

USS Forrestal on which Joe Monday served (photo), 31

vacation to Vietnam, 149

Valorous Unit Award, 114

Vasquez (Armando) and fellow Vietnam veteran Tom Bright, 232

Vasquez (Armando) later told me, "Not one wreath", 233

Vasquez (Armando) of San Angelo, Texas, helped start, 232

Index

Vasquez (Armando) served with the Army's, 232

Vasquez (Armando) to help start Concho Valley Vietnam Veterans, 233

Vasquez (Armando), Bright (Tom), and some other, 233

Vasquez(Armando) and Bright (Tom) attended a ceremony, 232

Vasquez, (Armando) "Some people say it's a healing", 232

Vasquez, Armando, 232, 233

Vasquez, Armando (photo), 232

VC may try to hit us, 121

VC were coming around back, 136

VC were the bad guys, 126

Veterans Day activities, 242

Veterans Day Parade (San Angelo, TX), 241, 242

Veterans Day Parade (San Angelo,TX), 241

Veterans Day Parade was in 1978, 241

veterans in Colorado City, Texas (photo), 219

Viet Cong, 114, 117, 120, 123

Viet Cong (VC), 121, 124, 125, 126, 136, 216, 217, 220

Viet Cong assassination squad, 125

Viet Cong hand grenade, 217

Viet Cong soldier running at me, 216

Viet Cong soldiers had tossed hand grenades, 124

Viet Cong were some of the worst terrorists, 126

Vietnam, 17, 18, 19, 22, 23, 26, 41, 58, 90, 92, 94, 99, 102, 105, 106, 107, 109, 110, 111, 112, 113, 114, 115, 117, 119, 120, 127, 131, 132, 134, 135, 136, 137, 141, 142, 144, 146, 148, 149, 150, 151, 154, 160, 162, 163, 164, 167, 168, 169, 170, 179, 183, 184, 196, 211, 216, 217, 218, 219, 220, 228, 232, 233, 236, 237, 238, 239, 240, 242

Vietnam (photo), 100, 101, 108, 109

Vietnam experience, 183, 214

Vietnam inside of me, 211

Vietnam Romance (poem), 184

Vietnam veteran, 179, 216

Vietnam Veteran of America, Chapter 457, 235

Vietnam veterans, 119, 170, 217, 218, 222, 227, 233, 234, 238, 240, 242, 243

Vietnam veterans as living reminders, 242

Vietnam veterans from the earlier years, 119

Vietnam veterans helping other Vietnam veterans, 217

Vietnam veterans in 2004, 241

Vietnam Veterans Memorial Moving Wall, 238

Vietnam Veterans of America (VVA), 231, 233, 235

Vietnam Veterans of America chaplain, 240

Vietnam Veterans of America helped donate, 239

Vietnam Veterans of America, Chapter 326, 240

Vietnam Veterans of America, Chapter 457, 232, 234, 239

Vietnam veterans of VVA 457, 240

Vietnam veterans responsible for the program, 234

Vietnam veterans started an organization, 233

Vietnam War, 26, 31, 46, 99, 122, 144, 168, 188, 218, 220, 227, 238

Vietnam War Memorial, 231

Vietnam War Memorial at Mathis Field, 234

Vietnam War memorial for San Angelo, 236

Vietnam War resulted in a major transition, 144

Vietnam War was a factor, 188

Vietnamese, 23, 139

Vietnamese Army, 134

Vietnamese citizen, 155

Vietnamese civilian, 123

Vietnamese clad in black clothing, 139

Vietnamese family, 124

Vietnamese girl, 126

Vietnamese girl whom Viet Cong, 123

Vietnamese lady was one of several "hooch maids" (photo), 109

V-Mail, 19

Vocational Industrial Clubs of America (VICA), 21, 22

voluntary participation, 69

volunteer for Jump School, 27

volunteer for Vietnam, 26

volunteered for Vietnam, 92

volunteering for Airborne, 13

Vomit Comet, 259

Vung Tau, South Vietnam, 114

VVA 457, 232, 236, 240, 243

VVA 457 had a chaplain, 240

Index

VVA 457 made me their new chaplain, 240

VVA 457 received it and placed it, 236

VVA Chapter 457, 242

W. F. Matthews: Lost Battalion Survivor, 229

W. F. Matthews: Lost Battalion Survivor (book), 229

Wackenhut Security Corporation, 188

Wackhenhut Corporation, 195

Waco, Texas, 21

waiting to board a C-141 Starlifter (photo), 207

Walker, (Marshall) the Director of Religious Activities (HSU), 186

Walker, Marshall, 186

Waller taught my fifth grade class, 14

Waller, Mr., 14

Waller's influence, 14

Ware (David) and I got involved in VICA, 22

Ware (David) outdid himself when he won, 22

Ware (David) served as chapter president, 22

Ware (David) served as parliamentarian, 22

Ware, David, 22

Ware, David (photo), 21

Warren (photo), during the opening assemblies, 200

Warren (Rick) sometimes invited members, 200

Warren, Rick, 200

Warren, Rick later became famous for his ministry, 200

Washington, 114, 182

WASP 2000, 226

WASP 2000 Reunion, 225

WASP reunion, 224

Way, Jim, 181

Wayland Baptist University, 177

Wayland Baptist University in Plainview, 177

Wayne, John, 25

Weekend Warriors, 61

West Texas, 37, 45

West Texas Museum, 103

West Texas University, 103

Western Airlines, 258, 259

Westmoreland (Gen. William C.) made a jump in Korea (photo), 170

Westmoreland (Gen. William C.) spoke to us, 170

Westmoreland, (Gen. William C.) who died during the, 171

Westmoreland, Gen. William C., 170

Westmoreland, Gen. William C. (photo), 170

What It Means to Be a Veteran (speech), 220

Wilkinson (Jack W.) died from "friendly fire", 147

Wilkinson (Jack W.) of the U. S. Navy, 146

Wilkinson, Camp, 146

Wilkinson, CMI Jack W., 146

Williams (Johnny Lawrence) served as a machine gunner, 19

Williams (L. J.) with an unidentified sailor (photo), 32

Williams family, 19

Williams, (L. J.), served in the Pacific, 20

Williams, Aunt Edna, 24

Williams, Johnny Lawrence, 19

Williams, Jr., (Richard L.) served in the Air Corps, 19

Williams, L. J., 20, 32

Williams, L. J. (photo), 32

Williams, L. J. saw action in the Pacific Theater, 32

Williams, Richard L., 19

Wilson, Flip, 196

Wilson, Jo, 151

Wilson, Treasure, 25

Wind Machine, 83

wings of a U. S. Army paratrooper (photo), 96

Wings Over Sweetwater (book), 224

Wings, WASP, & Warriors (book), 231

Winton, Carlton, 186

Winton's (Carlton) church in Frankfort, Kentucky, 186

Wisconsin, 240

Women Airforce Service Pilots (WASP), 86, 224, 225

Wood, Major Gen. Leonard, 51

Woodgate (Lt. Bruce) and I witnessed, 198

Woodgate (Lt. Bruce) had trained and qualified, 198

Woodgate, (Lt. Bruce) also attended seminary, 198

Woodgate, Lt. Bruce, 198

woods of Fort Campbell (photo), 175

World (United States of America), 119, 141

World Trade Center, 226

World War I, 17, 29, 167

World War II, 17, 19, 20, 32, 35, 68, 86, 144, 146, 159, 167, 192, 194, 222, 223, 224, 229, 231, 258

World War II aviation history, 231

World War II veterans, 222, 227

Yazzi, 150

You've Got a Friend (song), 151

Yuba Baptist Church (Yuba, OK), 212, 213

Yuba Baptist Church (Yuba, OK) (photo), 214

Yuba Baptist Church officially ordained, 213

Yuba, Oklahoma, 212, 213, 214, 215, 217

Zachry, (Juanita) gave me some much-needed, 184

Zachry, Juanita, 184

Zuni Indian from New Mexico, 150

www.ingramcontent.com/pod-product-compliance
Lightning Source LLC
Chambersburg PA
CBHW030229170426
43201CB00006B/155